Dougl
January, 2018

MW00379480

MULTIPLY

embrace a **life** of grace, community and mission

STEPHEN J. KIRK

MULTIPLY: embrace a life of grace, community and mission
Copyright © 2016 by Stephen Kirk
All rights reserved.

Requests for information should be addressed to:
Hope Church
4934 Western Row Road
Mason, Ohio 45040

Printed in the United States of America.

Dedication

To Amy, my precious wife, who partners with me daily
in the greatest adventure ever: discipling our children
into a life of grace, community and mission.
Partners, always.

Contents

Acknowledgments

At some level, while one author's name graces the cover, every book project is a team effort. One that attempts a comprehensive approach to the entire Christian life, all the more so. I must begin with my family. Thank you to my wife Amy for nearly 21 years of marriage and for serving as my primary sounding board as each chapter and theme of *Multiply* was born. Thank you for your insights and tweaks and for helping me remember the stories of our life that fill these pages. While not yet complete, our journey of making discipleship the centerpiece of our family life and our life together has been so meaningful and fulfilling. Thank you for serving as God's primary channel of grace and truth in my life. Thank you for believing that God had a book on discipleship that He wanted to write through me.

I also want to thank my seven children: Joshua, Emma Grace, Sophie, Abby, Caleb, Chloe, and Timothy. Not only have you inspired so many great illustrations, you have inspired me to keep pressing into God's grace, to keep growing as a father and as a man, and to keep learning how to see the life of Christ multiplied through me. Thank you for giving daddy up to put pen to paper. May *Multiply* serve as your guide into your life with Jesus, the community of saints He died to redeem, and the world around you He's eager to pursue through you. Mom and I are the richest people we know simply because you fill our lives with abundant joy.

To my mom and dad I say, "Well done!" Not that you raised a perfect son, far from it, but all along my journey you have pointed me to Jesus, you've reminded me of grace, you've demonstrated the steadfast love of God in countless ways, and you've made following Jesus look like the greatest kick anyone could enjoy! Your daily prayers for the entire Kirk family have been a living sacrifice and are bearing much fruit as your godly legacy unfolds. Keep growing and showing us all how it's done.

To the men and women who invested hours upon hours in my discipleship during my growing up years. There are literally too many to mention by name. But you probably know who you are. Thank you. I was always observing you and learning from your successes and failures, and from your joys and sorrows. How you handled yourself with grace and humility. I am so blessed when God gives me the gift of crossing paths with you only to discover that you are still following the same Jesus so many years later. Your abiding faithfulness spurs me on to stay faithful too.

To my Hope Church family in Mason, Ohio. Thank you for taking a risk on me as your senior shepherd eight years ago. I seek to never let a day go by where I presume upon your trust. I delight in you often as I pray for you and hear about all the many ways God is busy in you. He has us on this journey into multiplying discipleship together. Thank you for helping me weave grace into the fabric of our corporate family life. Thank you for never settling and always seeking to grow and mature into Christlikeness. Thank you for allowing God to stretch us all to have a greater measure of His heart for those who do not yet know Him. Living on mission isn't easy, but it's the best life possible and we have the privilege of helping each other get there. It's actually a blast!

Some specific helpers have partnered with me on this *Multiply* project. Thank you Jim Dunn for being a gifted, faithful partner in ministry. Like a Sherpa on Everest you've championed my pursuit of bringing multiplying discipleship back to the center of the local church. *"We'll get there!"* Thank you Patti Creutzinger for being a regular source of encouragement and a highly skilled assistant in ministry. Thank you Bill Craig for not only being my primary discipler in high school, but for the countless hours we spent architecting *Multiply*. If it were not for you, there would only be eight lifelong priorities! Ha! Thank you Hope Leadership Team for serving as the theological and practical incubator. Our collective insights have produced far more than I could have on my own. Thank you Barb Kuroff and Brenda Dunn for actually listening during English and grammar classes so that guys like me can write books like this. Your editorial insights were so helpful and encouraging. Thank you Shawn Davies for designing the *Multiply* logo, offering us visual learners four memorable shapes around which we can build the essence of the Christian life. From "nine rocks" on a napkin at Mason Grill to *Multiply*! And thank you Andy Haas for offering 30 different versions of the cover and allowing me to reject 29 of them without offense. You are a gracious artist. And finally, thank you Greg Ogden for your veteran affirmation of the viability of Triads (three men or three ladies covenanting to disciple together with the hope of eventual multiplication). My best experience in discipleship was a "Triad" even though we didn't know to call it that at the time. You gave it its nomenclature and have advocated for it as an effective strategy within the local church. Thank you.

Most importantly, thank you King Jesus for conquering death, pursuing me with relentless grace, and providing daily guidance through your Holy Spirit. You are the quintessential Discipler and we are all following You and modeling our lives after you. Apart from You, *Multiply* would simply sit as one man's pipedream. As it is, however, you are available and eager to bring the priorities of *Multiply* to life in all who dare to live in grace, with others, on mission! I humbly submit this project in your name, for Your glory, and for the lasting joy of all people.

INTRODUCTION

Welcome to *Multiply*! You're likely cracking open this book for one of two reasons: because your heart is stirred to get to know God; or because you're eager to be equipped to help others know God— whether for the first time or in a deeper way. My hope is that your motivation is a combination of the two reasons. And I believe you are in for a treat. With all the many things to which you could be giving your time and energy, this intentional investment will bring into focus the life for which God has made you. What could be more exciting than

discovering *who* **you are**
and *why* **you're here?**

From the beginning of creation, God's design is that our lives would be *multiplied*. In the Bible's first chapter we read God's missional call: *"Be fruitful, and multiply! (Genesis 1:28)"* In fact, God has written His story in such a way that His glory is multiplied when His character is reproduced in and through His people for the blessing of others. When people who do not know God come to know Him for the first time, and when those who know Him cultivate their relationship more purposefully and embrace His mission in His world, you get...*multiply*.

Now, no book can guarantee personal, spiritual growth or missional effectiveness. For two primary reasons. First, any and all growth in your character or in your capacity to reach others with Gospel grace is centrally dependent upon God's work in you and in others. A journey like this one is not like flipping on a light switch or waking up your smartphone. A journey like this one is not *"Do activity 'A' and guarantee result 'B' every time."* Rather, this journey is a process. And not always a clean one. Just like every other relationship in your life, there are many variables. And the X-factor in any spiritual endeavor such as *multiplying discipleship* is God Himself. His ways and thoughts are far higher than ours. So an important—and perhaps surprising—part of this journey is learning that we don't grow *for* God or work *for* God. Rather, by His grace and through His Spirit, He grows us and delights to work *through* us in the lives of others. So the pressure's *off* from the very beginning.

Which is *really* good news.

The second reason no guide can promise personal growth and multiplication is that *we* are the other main variable. God may be the prime mover, but we are participants—and we can be a bit fickle in our commitment. Our spiritual growth and missional effectiveness is God's work in us, but He doesn't force that work in reluctant individuals. We have to be willing to put in the time and effort. God has uniquely wired the whole process to be entirely dependent upon Him, while still requiring our willing engagement and faithful follow-through.

And *that* is indeed a mystery.

Sadly, many Christians aren't growing and aren't multiplying because they've lost sight of one of these two key ingredients. Either these believers have tried too hard in their own strength to be spiritual and effective and thus have grown weary, or they have become complacent and indifferent just waiting for God to prompt them. My encouragement and prayer for you as you begin this journey is that neither of these approaches would be your posture. Thankfully, getting to know God better, becoming more like His Son Jesus, and being used by God in the lives of others is not solely up to you. God is big enough, strong enough, and gracious enough to grow you there. And, He is also wise enough and kind enough to allow you to grow there at your own pace, involving you at every stage along the way. So at the end of this particular journey, as well as at the end of your life's journey, you will be able to say, *"That took everything I had!"* and also, *"Look what God did!"*

Oddly, but wonderfully, *both* will be true.

Now, why was *Multiply* worth writing, and why is this a journey worth taking? There are four reasons in particular: (a) to *specify* what it means to be a disciple of Jesus; (b) to *clarify* what matters most to Jesus; (c) to *give focus* to our praying; and (d) to *identify* what it takes to reproduce.

What it means to be a disciple of Jesus

First, how would you answer the question: *"What does it mean to be a Christian?"* Would you simply reference your belief that Jesus secured your eternal destiny by dying in your place for your sins? Or, would you also speak of a personal relationship with the living God, whom you engage daily, and are inviting to lead and guide you into the life He's designed for you? I've written *Multiply* because I'm concerned for future generations. Specifically, within the American Church, I'm afraid inadvertently we may be offering a Christian Gospel that enables one

**to be *saved* by Jesus
without becoming a *disciple* of Jesus?**

Perhaps born out of a correct desire to safeguard the Gospel from any notion of "works righteousness" or "earning one's salvation," somehow—and much to my chagrin—*faith* has been inappropriately separated from *following*. You will see as we go, I am rigorously committed to our personal salvation being a gift of God's grace through Jesus Christ alone. However, I simply cannot read the New Testament and draw the conclusion that Jesus is content with our intellectual acceptance of truth should that acceptance *not* result in a daily, personal relationship with Him, and ultimately, in life change. Jesus did not ask the initial disciples on the Sea of Galilee to merely acknowledge His existence. With gracious, compelling authority He called them to drop their nets and to follow Him the rest of their days. Their discipleship required a literal step of faith, not merely a preliminary, casual affirmation followed by a return to life as normal.

Saving faith clearly asserts that a real man from Nazareth named Jesus (who was the Son of God in the flesh) lived a God-honoring, sinless life, died an inhumane yet sacrificial death, experienced genuine bodily resurrection three days later, and now reigns in glory at the right hand of God offering forgiveness of sins and eternal life. Absolutely. I am banking the weight of my life on that good news! That same saving faith, however, is much more than a simple assertion. It is accompanied by a yielded, grateful posture of surrender. It is an *invitation*! An invitation for the now-risen King of glory

**to reign *over* and *in* and *through*
every nook and cranny of one's life.**

And this invitation is not optional extra credit reserved for those who are really radical about their Christian faith. Rather, it is intended to become a central component to *every* disciple's faith. This is why *Multiply* was worth writing. It is my attempt to cast a fresh vision for what it means to be a disciple of Jesus, providing a framework for what following Jesus with other disciples might look like.

What really matters to Jesus

Second, as disciples we need clarity on what matters most to Jesus. Whether we are new to Christian faith or have simply become inundated with a variety of disparate Christian messages, it is time to return to first things, simplifying what it means to be a disciple of Jesus in the 21st century. In Matthew 22:36 Jesus is asked to prioritize the greatest commandment.

His simple reply is: *love.*

Vertical love and horizontal love. Wholehearted devotion to God and sacrificial love for one's neighbor. Therefore, in *Multiply* I introduce nine *lifelong priorities* of a multiplying disciple, which elucidate these two expressions of love. These priorities are represented by four shapes to help make them memorable and reproducible. The first two shapes detail what it means to love God, while the second two shapes unpack what it means to love the people God places in our lives.

RECEIVE
Gospel Grace

LOVE
God as Father

HONOR
Jesus as King

FOLLOW
the Holy Spirit

LINK
deeply with a Few

DISCIPLE
together to Multiply

INVEST
in the Church

PURSUE
future Disciples

RESTORE
the Broken

Shape 1 – The STARTING POINT

Our first shape reminds us that *God alone has made it possible for us to be Jesus' disciples.* Being a disciple is all grace—and it's *always* grace. In other words, we start in grace at conversion, but we don't leave it there. Every single day, every step of the journey is a gift. That's what "grace" means: *gift.* So our engagement with God and participation in His mission throughout His world is never an attempt to earn His favor; rather, this engagement is our grateful answer to His grace at work in our lives.

We are *recipients*
before we are *participants.*

And we continue to RECEIVE God's grace as we follow Jesus together. Forgiveness from sin, wisdom, and power for a transformed life—these are gifts of grace that God delights to give us throughout our lives. We assigned grace its own shape because grace is so important, and sadly, because grace is so elusive for most of us. Everything within us wants to believe that grace is simply, totally a gift; however, we are conditioned to think we must earn or "deserve" virtually everything we receive—including grace. Thankfully, God delights to give grace freely, without condition.

Shape 2 – The STRONGER TRIANGLE

Our second shape reminds us that *our most important relationship is with the One who made us.* God made us for Himself, and He receives His due as we are joyfully content in Him and in His abundant provisions. Christianity is not a religion where rule-following and ritual-keeping is central; no, Christianity is a personal relationship with the living God that can be cultivated, transforming us from the inside out. The three sides of the Triangle remind us that although we relate to One God, this God has revealed Himself in history and through His Word as three persons—Father, Son, and Holy Spirit. Consequently, our relationship with God will grow as we learn to LOVE God as Father, HONOR Jesus as King, and FOLLOW the Holy Spirit into life.

Shape 3 – The CLOSER CIRCLE

Our third shape reminds us that *God has graciously given us companions for the journey.* A disciple's life with God is personal but was never intended to be kept private. God gives disciples of Jesus a special sibling bond. We share the same *redemption*, the same *Spirit* within us and among us, and the same *mission* in God's world. The Circle is divided into three parts to remind us that there are three primary ways we relate to one another in a local church. First, there are very intimate relationships that we can only have with a few (LINK) wherein deep knowing, vulnerability, and sacrifice find expression. Second, there are intentional relationships that form for a season (DISCIPLE) which are specifically aimed at spiritual growth and multiplication. And finally, there is our macro, corporate connection where we gladly INVEST our individual resources— time, talent, and treasure—for the blessing of the entire church family, our local community, and beyond.

Shape 4 – The FURTHER ARROW

Our final shape reminds us that *we have a mission!* At the start of His ministry, Jesus calls fishermen to follow Him. At the end of His ministry, just three years later, He sends them out into the world to make more disciples—Jesus *through* them. And they would do ministry as He did: pursuing men, women, and children with Gospel grace, and restoring brokenness as it crossed their path. His disciples were not peddlers of a product; they were ambassadors of a person…a King, a Redeemer. And so are we. Our mission is to offer those around us, through our words and our lives, a tangible experience of Jesus (PURSUE), while taking a genuine, compassionate interest in helping them flourish (RESTORE). God has placed people who are outside the faith inside our reach. Are we embracing the privilege of being a part of what God is doing in His world? We can.

While this is the natural order based upon the four shapes, you will notice that we have deliberately disrupted this order in the layout of the book in order to give you a taste of grace, community, and mission right out of the gate. We then unpack each of these themes as we go.

The word "lifelong" is intentionally selected. It would be easy to read through this book at a quick clip and become overwhelmed by all that God calls us to fold into our lives. This is why I encourage you to slow down and take your time. Read and reflect devotionally on each individual theme (four) under each priority (nine). These themes do not need to become your focus all at once over the next few weeks. Relax. God has given you a lifetime to reorient your priorities around His, and He is patient with those who are willing. As long as He gives you life, you will have opportunity to grow and deepen in each priority—some more than others in different seasons. Toward that end, I trust you will find this book helpful, as within it the nine priorities are clarified.

The importance of prayer

Perhaps a way to exhale, even as you begin *Multiply*, is to see these themes that matter most to God as themes He's committed to growing *in* you, rather than things you need to start doing *for* Him.

This journey will fail if it merely offers nine spiritual boxes for you to check in your own strength. Those who "do well" might end up feeling self-righteous, while those who struggle might end up exhausted and discouraged. Neither is a desired or acceptable result. Remember, being Jesus' disciple is first and foremost the cultivation of a growing relationship with the living God, not simply completing a religious "to-do" list. With this in mind, each of the nine priorities start with a prayer, which provides the framework for the four themes presented in every chapter. Daily prayer reminds us that this journey is about

**getting to *know* God,
not about doing stuff *for* Him.**

"Stuff" will come in time as He leads—really good, meaningful stuff; for He will equip you for everything to which He calls you. Prayer is a significant part of that equipping.

For a variety of reasons, consistent prayer is a challenge for most of us. Sometimes we simply forget to pray, sometimes we lose heart because our prayers aren't answered quickly or favorably, and sometimes it is just a matter of concentration. Our lives are so full of activity and pressure, decisions and deadlines, noise and sudden interruptions, that if we ever stop to pray we're often inundated with unrelated thoughts which make it difficult to remain mindful of the One to whom we're praying. *Multiply* offers you some "rails" to pray on—guiding you into a deeper, more deliberate prayer life. As you learn to pray daily for the things that matter most to God, I believe you will grow confident in His eager response. This is the promise we have from Jesus: *"Whatever you ask in my name, this will I do...if you ask me anything in my name I will do it"* (John 14:13-14). Far from inviting us to simply add "in Jesus' name" to the end of our prayers as a Christian version of *"Abracadabra,"* Jesus summons us to courageously pray for His will to be done. The apostle John confirms this: *"And this is the confidence we have toward Him* (Jesus) *that if we ask anything according to His will He hears us. And if we know that He hears us in whatever we ask, we know that we have the requests that we have asked of Him"* (1 John 5:14-15).

Prayer is a mystery to be sure, but at its heart it is a tangible way to connect personally with God—thanking Him for who He is and what He has done, and preparing your heart for what He is about to do in and through you. *A Disciple's Prayer* (found on the next page) has been written to guide you into this divine conversation. I encourage you to begin praying through it daily, and then living on the lookout for the surprising ways God chooses to respond. Discover the joy of participating in God's redemptive work all around you.

A Disciple's Prayer

RECEIVE   *God, thank You for Your pursuing grace that has found me and forgiven me!*

LOVE   *Father, show me Your love and enable me to love You with all of my heart, soul and mind.*

HONOR   *Jesus, lead me into a life of growing obedience, more today than ever.*

FOLLOW   *Holy Spirit, guide me and bear the fruit of Jesus' character in me today.*

LINK   *Equip me to love my spiritual brothers and sisters sacrificially as You have loved me.*

DISCIPLE   *Inspire me and enable me to disciple with others who will multiply.*

INVEST   *Motivate me to cheerfully and generously invest my time, energy, money and skills in my church.*

PURSUE   *Use me today to bring Gospel grace to those who are outside the faith but inside my reach.*

RESTORE   *Give me Your compassion and courage to play my part in restoring brokenness around me.*

I have joy in You and in the life You've given me.
Be glorified today…and appear soon!
Amen.

What it takes to reproduce

The fourth reason I wrote *Multiply* is that most Christian disciples have never been "discipled" by anyone and therefore wouldn't know quite where to begin if given a chance to disciple someone else. From the outside looking in, Jesus' plan to redeem the world appears very risky. Instead of waiting until the technology was in place and doing a live, worldwide interview on CNN, He chose to live largely in obscurity in the backwater towns of 1st century Palestine with 12 disciples. Day in and day out, He dined, walked with, and taught all of them, while giving concentrated time to three. He invested in them for three years. Then He sent them out to do with others what He had done with them—which was to prepare even more people to multiply. Like a pebble tossed in water,

Jesus launched a ripple-effect that
He designed to *reach* the ends of the earth.

And it has. And as long as Jesus' disciples partner with other disciples, helping one another grow and multiply, the ripple of Gospel grace will continue. If at any point along the way, however, disciples of Jesus settle for a consumer-driven Christian experience, wherein we only partake of events and programs that please our fancy, the ripple will stop.

Apparently you are catching this vision, because you are engaging with *Multiply*. My strong encouragement would be that you partner with a few people who, like you, want to grow and to become better prepared to take others on this discipleship journey. And these others will eventually be equipped to journey with others in the future. That is how multiply happens—when we intentionally prepare one another to reproduce reproducers:

disciples of Jesus who make other disciples of Jesus, who do the same. To that end, *Multiply* is intended to be experienced in the context of intimate Christian community. I recommend a Triad, a group of three guys or three ladies who covenant together to disciple with one another toward the goal of eventual multiplication. In fact, I highly recommend making your way through this book in a Triad, using the companion resource, *Multiply – Triad Guide*, which will guide your daily and weekly steps together.

Jesus' strategy to reach the world with Gospel grace is as follows: God's gift of pursuing grace launches our forever relationship with Him, which grows and flourishes in deep, authentic community, equipping and empowering us to live on mission at home, at work, and at play. Grace. Community. Mission. God Himself desires to live on mission *through* us. *This* is how He receives glory and intends to fill us with lasting joy.

Let's get started!

RECEIVE
Gospel Grace

"Father, Son, & Holy Spirit
thank You for Your pursuing grace that has
found me and forgiven me.

In view of Your grace, my sin grieves me
and I'm eager to turn from it.

I receive the Cross of Jesus that restores my fellowship with
You.

And I receive the Holy Spirit, who guarantees
that our fellowship will last."

1

RECEIVE

Gospel Grace

Pursuit – Repentance – Reconciliation – Guarantee

INTRODUCTION

It was the best Christmas, it was the worst Christmas. Well, it was the worst before it was the best. I was 12 and all I wanted was a brand new basketball hoop to replace the bent, rusty rim I had screwed into our oak tree. It had sufficed for a time, but it's time had passed. Finally Christmas morning arrived. I looked out back, but saw nothing. *"Uh oh,"* I thought. We then made it through all the gifts and no mention of a hoop. *"Uh oh"* turned into *"Oh, no."* But then my dad declared that there was one final gift. He said it was too big to be brought inside. Could it be? It *had* to be. You can imagine my anticipation. I shot up to look out the window, but my hopes were quickly dashed. It *was* a brand new basketball hoop—

the very one I had wanted, but my dad announced that it was *for* my little five-year-old niece, Sarah. It was the worst Christmas ever. At least for 20 seconds or so. And then my whole family (who were all in on it) announced with joy that the gift was actually for me. I was overcome with relief and delight. The worst became the best in a flash. I enjoyed that hoop immensely.

Do you have a similar memory? Did you ever receive a birthday present or a Christmas gift you'll never forget? What was it in particular that made it so meaningful? There is certainly something appealing and intriguing about opening a present. In the unwrapping, a secret treasure is unveiled to our joyful surprise, as we suddenly discover, either for the first time or in a new way, someone really knows us—what we appreciate and enjoy. Unlike a paycheck, gifts are not the earned by-product of *our* labor, they are the fruit of someone else's affection—*for us*. They aren't the required, proper compensation for services rendered. They are completely voluntary, only demanded by the glad fondness of the Giver for the beneficiary.

So it is with the Christian Gospel.

"Gospel" means "good news." And what makes the Christian news so good is that it is the announcement of the arrival of the greatest *gift* the world has ever been given. Unlike the dominant religions of our day, which are largely based on a human pursuit of the divine, the Christian Gospel proclaims *God's pursuit* of us. A mysteriously wonderful pursuit born, not out of a desire to *get* from us what He needs, but out of His passion to *give* us what He knows we need and long for most—Himself.

A central assumption behind the Christian Gospel is that we were made to know God, and that in knowing Him and honoring

His rightful place in our lives, we can actually become who He made us to be. I want to invite you to personalize that for a moment. In getting to know God and learning to honor His rightful place in your life, you can grow to become who He has made you to be. Put another way:

> **your capacity to *flourish* with a meaningful life is directly connected to your *experience* of God.**

Unfortunately, and difficult for us to admit, a proclivity to deliberately reject God and His will, and to seek out our identity, security, and purpose *apart* from Him is strong in us. This was true of the first humans, Adam and Eve, and it remains a consistent inclination for all of us. Despite the high levels of insecurity, fear, and disappointment that we're all too familiar with, we largely remain committed to a *self*-focused, *self*-sufficient lifestyle, wanting things our way and wanting to do them ourselves. *Does that sound familiar?* God certainly allows us to choose our own destructive desires over Him, but He also eagerly extends abundant grace, knowing that real life is found only in Him.

"Grace," or the Greek word *charis*, literally means "gift." To our surprise, even in the face of our rejection, God leans in, leans toward us in the person of Jesus Christ in order to give us the gift of Himself. And He is not a reluctant redeemer. It is God's great joy to take our warranted judgment for our sin upon Himself, giving rebels like us the undeserved blessings of forgiveness, relationship, presence, and hope. If we'll receive them.

If we'll receive *Him*!

Just like opening your hands prepares you to receive a present from a friend, confessing your desperate need for grace opens your heart to receive God. And if you turn to Him, He will never reject you. He delights to restore you to Himself and to anchor your heart in His unfailing love. Our exhausting pursuit of life apart from God finally rests in accepting His gracious pursuit of us.

Have you accepted this gift of being *found*?

Receiving Gospel grace is the *starting point* of your life-long journey of following Jesus. Instead of trying to convince God that we are worthy to be numbered among His disciples, God, through the life, death, and resurrection of Jesus, convinces us of His confounding, yet wonderful love. And He gladly applies His grace over and over again as our hearts are often slow to take it in. Your initial receiving is called "conversion," and in that moment you are mercifully saved from God's fair justice against *all* the sins you've already committed and *all* your sins that lie ahead. That is hard to believe. But think about it: if you had to pay for your sins or right all the wrongs yourself, saving you wouldn't be a gift, would it? With the God revealed in the Bible, it's a gift.

It is *always* a gift.

And when you receive it initially, you find yourself rightly wanting to receive it afresh every day thereafter. Not because you go in and out of being "saved," but simply because you want to stay current with your Savior. After all, being a disciple of Jesus is a relationship, not a religion. So, keeping short accounts with Him by regularly owning your sin and receiving fresh expressions of grace from God's hand cultivates the rapport and strengthens the bond. It reminds you of your great need and God's boundless sufficiency. As the prophet Jeremiah says, *"The steadfast love of the Lord never ceases; His mercies never come to an end; they are new every morning; great is your faithfulness"* (Lamentations 3:22-23). Wow. Every new day that dawns is filled with new mercy.

Breathe **that in and come** *alive.*

The Gospel good news is that God is always faithful even when we aren't, and He is more committed to us than we ever will be to Him. So receive Gospel grace with gratitude, confidence, and humility. These are proper, daily postures of a growing disciple. Humbled both by your own sin and God's grace, you can confidently acknowledge your need for God and thank Him for His pursuit. A pursuit John Newton captured so well in 1779 with the writing of perhaps the most famous English hymn, *"Amazing grace, how sweet the sound that saved a wretch like me. I once was lost, but now am found, was blind but now I see."* Found. That is such an encouraging thought. Found by the One who made us, the One from whom we've been hiding for too long. We never outgrow our need for grace. Thankfully, God never outgrows His desire to give it. Can you open your hands? Can you open your heart? Are you ready to receive and begin *again*? God is. God is ready. Always.

PURSUIT

When I was about three years old my favorite toy was a "Big Wheel." It was really just a glorified plastic tri-cycle, but it sat low to the ground, which made you feel like you were a motor-cross daredevil. One spring evening my brother Tim—16 years old at the time—went to our church's High School youth group meeting. I was upset because I wanted him to stay home and play wiffleball with me instead. What three-year-old isn't a naïve narcissist? I decided to remedy the situation by hopping on my self-propelled hot rod and showing up at church. *"Surely Tim would have to concede if I made such an effort,"* I thought. It was about a half-mile ride, which is a lot on a Big Wheel. The distance, however, was the least of my worries. I had to cross over a busy four-lane road in order to complete the journey. Honestly, I don't even remember doing it, but what I do remember is the look of relief on my sister's face as she found me at church. My buddy Carlos had bailed on me a few minutes into our ride and returned home to tell my folks that I had left. Their feverish search began in earnest. Because they loved me. Having exhausted all reasonable options, they finally discovered me virtually aloof in the Fellowship Hall. I certainly didn't know how dangerously lost I was, nor how valuable, until I was found by their tenacious pursuit and experienced their joy in retrieving me.

And so it is with receiving Gospel grace.

Through Old Testament prophets, priests and Kings with Israel, and supremely through the person of Jesus Christ in the first century, God eagerly pursued lost humanity in order to find us and restore us to Himself. No passage in the New Testament captures the tenacity of this gracious pursuit more than Luke 15. The context is the key to understanding this dramatic episode. The Jewish religious leaders accuse Jesus of *receiving* and *dining* with "tax collectors and sinners." This is a summary title for the despised outcasts of first century Palestine. The majority of the "religious" considered these individuals unworthy of their presence and intentionally avoided contact with them.

But *not* Jesus.

Knowing that these sinners had been made in the image of God, believing that they were unaware of their true value and their "lostness," Jesus intentionally pursues them with grace. In fact, as God-in-person, Jesus' willingness to share a meal with the discarded was God personally initiating a relationship. It is no surprise that Jesus became known as the *"friend of sinners"* (Matthew 11:19).

To make His point, Jesus tells a parable with three metaphors communicating one theme: *God's pursuing grace.* A shepherd that discovers one of his sheep has been lost searches as far as he must in order to find it and bring it home, even leaving the other 99 to retrieve the one. This seems unreasonable to us, but that one sheep is more valuable to the shepherd than we can imagine. Similarly, a woman who misplaces a precious coin, rather than dismissing it as expendable, diligently scours her entire home until she finds it. She erupts into explicable rejoicing in its recovery. You know that feeling when you simply cannot find your wallet or your phone or your most prized piece of jewelry. And then someone breaks the growing tension, *"Found it!"* Oh, the relief. Obviously, for Jesus the ecstatic joy of both the shepherd and the woman parallels God's joy in finding us!

Finding *you*.

Whenever you accept being found—turning from your sin and receiving Gospel grace either for the first time or in a fresh way—there is great rejoicing. Remember, God is not a reluctant redeemer. He is *inclined* to show you mercy. His redemptive pursuit is His great delight. Jesus shatters our man-made caricatures of God that have Him aloof and disinterested. He is like a shepherd looking behind every bush for his lamb or a woman looking in every crevasse for her most valuable possession.

Now, all of this sets the stage for the third and profound metaphor of a loving father pursuing a lost son. This is where Jesus gets even more personal. Prideful and selfish, the son grieves his dad and shames his family by running away and squandering a prematurely demanded inheritance. He shouldn't even have been given it ahead of his father's passing, but his father gives over to the son's foolish, stubborn proposal. Perhaps the father knew his son would need to experience personal lack before he could recognize the gracious provision readily available in his father's home. Eventually, having run out of options and realizing that even his father's slaves have it better back at the ranch, he begins to scheme his way back into the village. Though logical, he deceives himself into believing he must *earn* his way home. We are all vulnerable to a similar approach to God. Having become aware of our own rebellion, it is natural for us to presume that we must overcome the deficit and "worthy" ourselves. God has a different way. One that actually works.

Unbeknownst to the son, the faithful, loving father pursues his lost boy. *"While he (the son) was still a long way off,"* the father saw him, felt compassion for him, ran to him, embraced him, and kissed him (Luke 15:20)! Literally it says that the father fell on the neck of his son. Can you picture that? The Father tackling the son with love. How utterly shocked must the poor, pathetic boy have been? Imagine if it were you. What emotions would have flooded your heart?

Relief? Gratitude? Joy?

The son has no chance to make it to town or to reveal his plan for redeeming himself by earning back the inheritance he wasted. He is simply stunned and overwhelmed, both physically and emotionally, by undeserved grace. What he doesn't know is His grateful father is just getting started. After retrieving his son, he blesses him, decks him out with the very best clothes, and throws a party in his honor. Not because—and this is the critical point—his lost son came home, but because *"he was lost and is found!"* (Luke 15:32).

The common thread that ties together the three metaphors in Jesus' story is the tireless pursuit of something that doesn't know its real value. The religious leaders couldn't understand why Jesus would sup with sinners. Jesus wouldn't have it any other way. Jesus is God the Father in gracious, persistent pursuit of lost sons and daughters, like you and me. Perhaps challenging for your heart to believe, to the One who made you, you are that valuable sheep, coin...child.

We simply don't know *who* we are
because we don't know *whose* we are.

You might read that again. That thought has been one of the most life-changing for me. It is illustrated in Disney's blockbuster movie *Tangled*, where year after year on their kidnapped daughter's birthday the King and Queen send out lighted, floating lanterns hoping to draw their daughter home. Year after year, from her prison-like tower she sees them, but doesn't know their source or their significance. Finally, when given a chance to escape, she makes her way to the origin of the lanterns, only to discover that they lead her home. Her home, where she sees her likeness in the queen's face, and discovers for the first time that she has been a princess all along. This is a bit of what happens when you receive God's pursuit through Jesus Christ. You discover who you really are. Royalty.

Why do we scramble around so much trying to fill our lives with things other than God, things we think will satisfy our heart's deepest desires? They never do. Not ultimately at least. They may for a time, but the quenched thirst is temporary, and eventually we feel empty and thirsty again. It's an exhausting treadmill that never leads anywhere. It's like we're lost and we can't find our way home. Thankfully, there is a Father in pursuit, ready to fall on our necks with redemptive grace! Are you ready to receive? Are you longing to be found? You can be. Let gratitude rise in your heart today in response to this good news.

REPENTANCE

One of the lousiest memories of being a kid is being caught in a "crime" and trying to wiggle out of it to no avail. A friend and I once decided it would be amusing to roll up a newspaper, light the end of it, and smoke it like a big, fat cigar. The imprudence of the moment was only magnified by our location at the time. We were in my parent's bathroom. Needless to say, the little flame became huge in about 2.4 seconds, and I had a blazing torch in my hand that needed to be extinguished. My friend couldn't get the window open (as if throwing it out on the roof would have been a good solution) so in desperation I chucked it into the toilet. Good news? Fire was extinguished. Bad news? It melted and charred the seat on its way out. Conveniently for my friend, his mom arrived at that very moment and whisked him away. I was left holding the bag. I had a decision to make. Would I own my infraction or deny it? I went with denial initially, but as you can imagine, my folks saw right through the implausibility. While I was stringently disciplined, my guess is my parents had at least a brief chuckle about the whole episode.

With seven kids, my wife and I have had many opportunities for such humorous moments. One in particular happened on a Sunday morning. When you're a pastor's family, stuff always seems to happen on Sunday morning. I was off to church early and Amy discovered one of our children completely covered in marker. Sharpie marker. Black...Sharpie...marker. It was everywhere. And predictably, with twinkling eye and a puzzled face that seemed shocked we would accuse her, that sweet child completely denied any direct interaction with a Sharpie marker. Ha!

And we laugh. Yet, as adults are we really all that different when it comes to our own sin? Somehow we convince ourselves that God doesn't know. That He doesn't "see" the marker. The stains from all our choices and cover-ups. Yet Scripture couldn't be clearer: *"The Lord searches every heart and knows every plan and thought"* (1 Chronicles 28:9). While we can only see the polished exterior, God sees deep within. This is why it is so important that we learn the art of owning our sin with Him. Somehow, we convince ourselves that, if we just skip that part, everything will be ok.

But actually it's in being *emptied*
through humble confession
that your heart is prepared to be *filled*
with forgiving grace.

It is a gift to our bodies that we feel a burn when we touch the stove, or a shock when we touch an outlet in the wall. In the same way, it is a gift to our hearts when we feel a healthy grief over our sin. It is normal to ache internally over your sin, admitting that you fall far short of God's best—the glory, for which you were originally made. The apostle Paul explains, *"I rejoice, not because you were grieved, but because you were grieved into repenting. For you felt godly grief...(which) produces a repentance that leads to salvation without regret"* (2 Corinthians 7:9-10). As the found son from Luke 15 cried out, *"Father, I have sinned against heaven and before you. I am no longer worthy to be called your son"* (Luke 15:21). That's godly grief. Whenever we choose our own way—rejecting what God *has* provided by reaching for and seizing what He *hasn't*—God laments. Thankfully, His grief prompts an even greater pursuit! And in the safety of His tenacious love, we can own our sin and receive His forgiveness. *"...God's kindness is meant to lead you to repentance"* (Romans 2:4). Godly grief readies us for a second response.

The Greek word translated as "confess" means "to agree." In our convicted grief we acknowledge that we have wrongly chosen *our* way over God's. This is a good start. Yet, in order to complete our confession, we also need to acknowledge our deep longing to move in God's direction...*again*. Interestingly, the Hebrew word for "repent" is the simple word "turn." It describes the deliberate *pivot* a hiker makes when he realizes he's gone off course. Time to reroute and get back on track.

Repentance is our *spiritual pivot*.

Throughout the Christian life there is great grace for this "turn." God delights in you when you declare your desire to *return* to the course He has chosen for you.

This is true initially in conversion, but this remains true all throughout our journey with Jesus. Regular confession, even daily, is a healthy practice for a growing disciple. Has it been a while since you grieved over your sin? What do you think keeps you from going there? Are you completing your confession by deliberately turning *from* your sin and *toward* God's best again? As risky as repentance may seem, it is God's gracious way of restoring you to Himself and helping you move forward again into life.

In Psalm 51 King David offers us a beautiful example of godly grief and a strong desire to embrace God's way again. The prevailing metaphor is like a bath after a long day's work in the yard. Before a pure and holy God, David feels "dirty." David *is* dirty. He's committed adultery and attempted to cover his tracks by murdering his mistress' husband. And God is deeply grieved. But He is also deeply committed to David. So, He convicts David's heart, bringing him to an uncomfortable yet critical place of brokenness. David faces a life-changing fork in the road. He can either keep running in the wrong direction—attempting futilely to "manage" his brokenness, or He can turn back into grace.

He *chooses* grace.

He cries out, *"Have mercy on me, O God"* (Psalm 51:1)! This bold request isn't born of David's desert, but because he believes in God's steadfast love. Our confidence before God is never about *our* faithfulness. It is always about God's faithfulness. Confidently David pleads, *"Blot out my transgressions. Wash me thoroughly from my iniquity, and cleanse me from my sin! Purge me...and I shall be clean; wash me and I shall be whiter than snow. Create in me a clean heart, O God"* (Psalm 51:1-2, 7, 10). Poetically choosing about every Hebrew word for "make clean," David understands that his only hope is God's great mercy. Though on a human level, having all power and authority as Israel's king, David is incapable of washing away his own sin! We all are.

Thankfully, God is *able*!

And more than able, God is willing. Always. *Willing*. That's an important part of David's prayer too. He knows that true repentance is not just feeling sorry for a brief moment and moving on, but yielding his will to God's will in a new way. *"...renew a right spirit within me. Restore to me the joy of your salvation, and uphold me with a willing spirit"* (Psalm 51:10, 12). David recognized that God's way would be best, but he also suspected it wouldn't be easy. So he asked for assistance. Is that your prayer? Wanting God's best is a start, but do you find yourself asking God to help you get there? This invitation—confessing your need for God—opens the door for real movement from within. Are you willing to give God access to the deepest parts of you? He's ready.

RECONCILIATION

"Religion" has been around since the beginning of time. No matter the culture, humanity consistently develops a concept of the divine. There's almost a universal awareness that there is something or someone *greater*. Increasingly, many assume this so-called "god" is a therapeutic, non-judgmental, soft pushover, who exists merely to keep us content and happy. Others, however, perceive "god" to be impersonal and detached. For the Eastern pantheist, "god" is like a force that is in everything from the inanimate to the living—rocks and trees and birds alike. So he may be "nearby" in one sense, but "god" is certainly not available or interested in a relationship. It is pretty difficult to relate personally to "energy."

The Western deist suffers from the same problem, but for a different reason. They locate "god" as somewhere far away, aloof and unaffected by the everyday happenings on the earth or in our lives. He may have made the world, but, like a watch-maker from the early 1900's, he merely "wound" it up and is now watching it wind down, playing more the role of spectator than participant. This "god" is indifferent. Even if he could do something to help, he might choose not to anyway. Unlike the pantheist "god," the deist "god" is nowhere close. Yet, *like* the pantheist "god," the deist "god" is unavailable and uninterested in relating at a personal level.

If we were to note a fourth common view of "god," it would probably be one who has great power, but who is often arbitrarily angry with humanity. Due to His unpredictability, people often pursue religious activity in an effort to keep him appeased or pacified. Comparatively speaking, as long as we are not dramatically worse than our neighbor and are able to maintain a modicum of morality or ethics, we assume that "god" is obligated to make our life go well. Therefore, if life isn't going as we had hoped, we either assume "god" is at fault and worthy of our neglect—and we disengage, or we ramp up our religiosity hoping to earn our way back into "god's" good favor, which merely delays our indifference. Can you relate to some variation of one of these perspectives? A grandpa-like Santa in the sky? An impersonal, mysterious force? An emotionally numb, apathetic being? An unpredictably capricious "god?" Subtly, these have great influence in our world today.

The "god" revealed in the Bible, however, offers a completely different perspective. He cannot be contained "in" nature as He alone is the One who created all things and is sovereign over all things. Yet in his sovereignty, the biblical God is not emotionally cool or detached.

He is highly *personal* **and involved.**

And while completely and solely worthy of our awe, the God revealed in the person of Jesus is also a passionate God committed to personal relationship. When the pursuing father received the rebel boy in Luke 15, it wasn't to hire him back as a servant; it was to *restore* him as a son! And so it is with us. Since God is holy and righteous and good, our rejection of Him cannot be dismissed as inconsequential, or simply overlooked. Yet, because God is gracious our rejection *can* be overcome. This is Gospel grace:

God's justice takes our sin *seriously.*
God's love takes our sin *personally.*

That is, God takes away our sin by personally absorbing the due penalty our sin deserves. This is why the most iconic, central symbol of the Christian faith is a Roman cross. In the person of Jesus Christ and through His self-emptying, sacrificial death, God arrives to take away our sin. He keeps His New Covenant promise from the prophet Jeremiah, *"I will forgive their iniquity and remember their sin no more"* (Jeremiah 31:34). Or as King David declares, *"...as far as the east is from the west, so far does he* (God) *remove our transgressions from us"* (Psalm 103:12). God does not intervene on our behalf simply to "hire" us to work for Him, He graciously intervenes to forgive us all our sin and to restore the original fellowship our sin shattered. Through Jesus, God gladly reconciles us to Himself, reestablishing a forever relationship with us, which we were made to have. Only God's grace can redeem what our sinful rebellion forfeits. And God is pleased to redeem.

In Romans 5:8 the apostle Paul explains that God did not wait for us to get our act together—to be *worthy* of saving—but instead God lovingly took the initiative to die for us *"while we were still sinners."* In fact, Paul acknowledges that God's love overcame our active rebellion—*"we were enemies"*—by reconciling us to Himself through the death of Jesus (Romans 5:10). Think about it: Who on earth eagerly restores fellowship with their enemies?

Gospel grace is *baffling,*
but not *bewildering.*

Its perplexity induces our intrigue. Paul affirms a similar thought in 2 Corinthians 5:18-19, *"...through Christ God reconciled us to Himself...that is, in Christ God was reconciling the world to Himself, not counting their trespasses against them."* Consider your own life for a moment. Wouldn't you be willing to reconcile with someone who wounded you deeply as long as they were genuinely repentant and willing to repair the damage? Now, imagine if they were unwilling and incapable of restitution. This is our posture and plight before God. Stubborn and inept. Willful and powerless. Yet, God still reconciles. He is the wounded party as we each find numerous ways to shun His glory. Yet, He initiates reconciliation and provides the means of repair Himself, even providing *Himself* as the means of repair. *"And you, who once were alienated and hostile in mind, doing evil deeds, He (God) has now reconciled in His body of flesh by His (Jesus) death, in order to present you holy and blameless and above reproach before Him"* (Colossians 1:21-22).

It's all grace!

Always.

Does your heart believe it? You were made to be in personal, intimate fellowship with the living God, knowing Him and being known by Him. How does that strike you? What emotions does that evoke? What questions does it raise for you? The word "reconcile," both in English and in the original biblical Greek, means "to put *back* together." So imagine the profundity of this gracious act. In calling you through the Gospel, God *is* inviting you into something new, but not something totally foreign. He's recovering a previous reality — a relationship He once enjoyed in the beginning, with humanity — Adam and Eve, in Eden. And God is so eager to restore the fellowship, He allows Himself to be broken — through the Cross — so that we can be put back together. Ironically, as the wounded party,

He takes our *brokenness*
so that we might experience His *wholeness*,

and enjoy fellowship with Him forever. As the prophet Isaiah says in anticipation of the coming Messiah — Jesus, *"But he was wounded for our transgressions...upon him was the chastisement that brought us peace, and with his stripes we are healed"* (Isaiah 53:5). No one can reconcile him/herself to God. But God can. And through Jesus' Cross He did. It is His great joy to extend this most abundant gift. No wonder Paul delightfully proclaims, *"we rejoice in God through our Lord Jesus Christ, through whom we have now received reconciliation"* (Romans 5:11). Received. Is that true for you? Have you received? Does your heart rejoice? If so, take some time to tell God all about it. And if not, you might ask God to fill you with wonder at this compelling news. Your ears will never hear a more comforting, once-and-for-all affirmation: *"Reconciled."* Life has a way of breaking us. We have a way of breaking ourselves. God has a way—and God alone—of putting us back together. Invite Him to put you back together.

GUARANTEE

In the film *Amazing Grace,* there's a climactic scene where stubborn Wilberforce finally allows the grace of God to light upon his heart. His chef finds him lying in the grass in the garden almost gleeful and asks, *"Have you found God, sir?"* To which Wilberforce rightly and joyfully responds, *"No. I think He's found me!"* And that's how it goes when you decide to follow Jesus. "Decide" is an interesting word. There *is* a movement of our will to be sure, but receiving Gospel grace is less about us moving our will and more about our will being *moved.*

God's grace is *that* powerful.

When it sets in, you are moved from being lost, condemned, and broken to being found, forgiven, and restored. And all you care to say is, *"Yes."*

And when you finally do, you discover the surprising wonder that fellowship with God is for keeps. It lasts. Since most human relationships ebb and flow circumstantially—some even stopping suddenly over the pettiest of self-concern—most of us operate on the principle: "once bitten, twice shy." Thankfully with God there is no comparable uncertainty. Since God is predictably unchanging and eternal Himself—existing before anything was ever created— your new fellowship has an *eternal* quality right out of the gate. It *begins* and is developed in this life, but it continues uninterrupted whenever this life is through. Which is an amazing hope. When you receive Gospel grace you receive the heart-anchoring *assurance* that life with God outlasts everything else. The Apostle Paul reinforces this truth in Romans 8:38-39, *"For I am sure that neither death nor life, nor angels nor rulers, nor things present nor things to come, nor powers, nor height nor depth, nor anything else in all creation, will be able to separate us from the love of God in Christ Jesus our Lord."* I shared this verse one evening with my then seven year old daughter and she gently challenged it, *"So...you're saying nothing can?"* Her nine year old brother responded, *"Yeah. That verse covers everything!"* I smiled. She smiled. I could visually see assurance beginning to anchor her heart.

But how can we know *for sure*?

Since most of our lives are filled with a litany of broken promises and shattered dreams, our hearts are not so easily convinced. Are we to just take God at His word, or is there something substantial that we can rest in? Well, yes and yes. "Faith" certainly takes God at His Word—and Scripture is filled with many great promises to believe—but God is also eager for us to really know and experience this hope ahead of time. So, He's chosen to place His very own Spirit within us as a *guarantee* that our relationship is unbreakable, and that far, far more is on the way!

In Ephesians 1:3-14, like a waterfall of good news—one run-on sentence in the original Greek—the apostle Paul highlights God's unwavering commitment to His own children. Allow it to wash over you and refresh you. On account of Jesus' Cross and resurrection, and through your trusting relationship with Him, God delights...

to *bless* you with every spiritual blessing,
to *choose* you before the foundation of the world,
to *predestine* you for adoption in love,
to *redeem* you through His blood,
to *forgive* your sin,
to *lavish* His grace upon you,
and to *reveal* to you His will to unite all things in Christ.

And all of this without you lifting a finger to earn it.

**Oh, if only our hearts were willing to *rest*
in the truth of these words every day!?**

Paul completes this soul-enlivening cascade by promising an eternal inheritance that we will one day possess. So eager for us to know for sure, God *seals* us *"with the promised Holy Spirit, who is the guarantee of our inheritance"* ahead of time (Ephesians 1:14). Similarly, Paul says in 2 Corinthians 1:21-22, *"And it is God who establishes us with you in Christ...and who has also put His seal on us and given us His Spirit in our hearts as a guarantee."* Or again, in 2 Corinthians 5:5, *"He who has prepared us for this very thing is God, who has given us the Spirit as a guarantee."* In other words, God wants you to live every moment from this day forward with constant assurance, so He places His very own presence—His Holy Spirit—*within* you as a guarantee. And this guarantee is forever. As Paul affirms, *"...by whom* (the Holy Spirit) *you were sealed for the day of redemption"* (Ephesians 4:30).

In Greek the word for "seal" refers to the imprint of a King's ring set in wax over the fold of a letter. This seal declared to all parties both that the letter belonged to the King and that its contents could never be tampered with without reprisal. According to Paul,

God—the King above all kings—treats His own children with the same concern. God, the Holy Spirit is the sign of ownership and protection. His presence within us is God's seal on our hearts, signifying that in fact we belong to God and that we always will. *Always*. In a world of such flux, "always" is a very encouraging word.

The Spirit is God's *guarantee*.

The Greek word *"arrabon"* refers to a down-payment, a first installment that promises *"More is on the way."* This transaction happens every day as new home owners put down 20% on a mortgage. It's not the total amount, but it is real money and a binding promise that the other 80% will come in due time. Even today in Modern Greece an *"arrabon"* is the engagement ring a hopeful groom gives his fiancée. It is a tangible symbol of their current relationship *and* a pledged promise that even more is on the horizon. God doesn't want you wondering another day whether or not you belong to Him, nor if your fellowship will last. The Holy Spirit within you is His pledge, the first installment of your real inheritance and a tangible promise that there is more to come.

Have you ever acknowledged the personal presence of God's Spirit within you and known the *certainty* the Spirit intends to provide? We will explore that more together in chapter six. In the meantime, however, rest perhaps for the first time in Gospel grace. You might even take a literal deep breath right now and exhale slowly and rest. Inhale for four seconds, hold for four seconds, and exhale for four seconds. Do you know that our spiritual lives desperately need that restful pace as well?

Grace is your soul's *exhale*.

Breathe in and *breathe out* the truth of God's grace. You can never be noble enough to deserve it, nor corrupt enough to lose it.

Breathe *in*, breathe *out*.

It's not about the quality of *your* character, but the quality of God's character.

Breathe *in*, breathe *out*.

It's not about your capacity to make things right, but about God's unrivaled aptitude and abundant joy which have already seen to it. Because of Jesus things are already right.

Breathe *in*, breathe *out*.

Receive, and rest. It's not about your faithfulness to your vow, it's about trusting God to keep His promises. He is the faithful One. Rejoice in His faithfulness. Bank the weight of your life on His faithfulness. And watch your heart well up with thanksgiving.

If God is worthy of anything, it is our growing, daily, throughout-the-day gratitude. Do you find that stirring and surging inside? If so, be assured Gospel grace *is* making its way, making its home deep within you. God Himself is making His home deep within you. Are you getting to know Him? Are you eager to know Him better? That's what this *Multiply* journey is all about. And this journey works best if you share it with a few others. What would it look like for you to link deeply with a few Christian siblings who are likewise discovering the freeing, anchoring, transforming grace of the Gospel? Let's explore LINK together.

LINK
deeply with a Few

DISCIPLE
together to Multiply

INVEST
in the Church

"Father, Son, & Holy Spirit
thank You for giving me the gift of spiritual siblings.

Equip me to love them sacrificially as You have loved me.

Use me to help them love, honor, and follow You.

Give me the courage to own my sin with them
and to extend your grace to them."

2

LINK

deeply with a Few

Family – Sacrifice – Encouragement – Vulnerability

INTRODUCTION

Fall in the Midwest has always been one of my favorite times of the year, and one of the things I've always loved about the Fall is Halloween. It was the only time of year when you could dress up like a favorite superhero and walk around in public without the threat of ridicule. In fact, everyone always "loved" your costume...even if they didn't. And were those masks not the most awesome invention? There was nothing like having a nasty smelling, hard plastic facade strapped to your face with a stapled rubber-band cutting off the circulation in the top of your ears. Sure, it was a vice for your face, but you got free candy for your trouble!

Whether I was Batman, Spiderman, The Incredible Hulk, or my favorite Dallas Cowboy player, every costume had one thing in common: a *mask*. For an hour-and-half you got the delightful chance to look like and to act like somebody else. And that was fun. But as I've grown up and become the adult on the inside of the great candy exchange, I realize that all the candy-hander-outers throughout my childhood were wearing masks too. Except for them, "Mask-day" wasn't a holiday; it was pretty much every day of the year. And *this* is the central reason we find it difficult to relate well with others.

It's these darn *masks* that get in the way.

While each of us is a product of different relational environments, we all learn early the art of *playacting*; taking our cues from those around us. We aren't given a handbook for this, but like on-the-job-training we observe what we are *allowed* to feel and which emotions are unacceptable. For example, some family systems don't allow tears as it's a sign of weakness. If you grew up in this environment, you may have learned to *stuff and bluff*.

You may naturally hide the *real* you
because it's not safe to be *exposed*.

Since *exposure* is such a strong fear, you may decide it's better to remain anonymous than to risk being known. *"What if they don't like the genuine 'me'?"* Of course the irony of this perspective is that it keeps you in control—which *feels* good, but tends to lead to few if any relationships. And the ones you *do* find, tend to be a bit shallow and superficial. You *want* to be known, but it's just easier to wear the mask.

I say "easier," but honestly, just like on Halloween, it can be a bit suffocating behind the mask. Our genuine self struggles to breathe, but we keep convincing ourselves that it's safer *in hiding*. Can you relate to this at all? Have you ever taken the time to reflect on your family system and how it continues to influence your relationships as an adult? It's not about finding fault in your parents or siblings; it's about putting some of the pieces together. In the end, we all make our *own* choices when it comes to donning our masks.

Fear of exposure leads to many masks. There is another fear, however, that has influenced many of us to become professional bluffers as well: *rejection*. Maybe you courageously stuck your neck out at some point and shared the real you only to find others walking away. You don't have to experience that more than once or twice before you become a stock-holder in *Disguise Inc.* Or, perhaps you thought you were embraced for your honesty, only to discover that others had welcomed you publically but were spurning you privately. I fear that many of us were wounded by a form of gossip in our early days and we have never really recovered. We're older now, but the fear of being rejected has trumped the fear of exposure. So, we just punt relationally; convincing ourselves that it's not worth the hassle or the risk. We have one life to live; what might we be missing out on?

Oh, and one final reality check. Difficult for us to admit, but all of us to some degree have to come to terms with the fact that we have become accustomed to the *persona* we've created. Initially, the mask doesn't portray who you really are. It's foreign. But in time, unchecked, it becomes more familiar to you than just being you.

**Many aren't even sure *who* they are,
because they've been masquerading for so long.**

We adjust to this person and that one, depending on the situation, which is exhausting. And worse, as I said earlier, it's suffocating. Your real self forgets how to breathe. Part of the gift of Gospel grace, receiving it and becoming a part of a family with grace coursing through its veins, is that you can finally drop the weighty façade and exhale. Don't you long for that? God intends for you to experience it with a few others. Let's discover how, together.

FAMILY

One of my fondest memories as a parent occurred at about 11:30 one summer night. I was stumbling up to bed pretty exhausted and, as I neared the top stair, I noticed the voice of my eldest daughter, who was eight at the time. My initial thought was that she and her sister were disobeying by staying up well beyond their bedtime, talking. They had been sneaking this, but promised us that they would end at nine. So I was a bit miffed by their brazen disregard. I geared up for the confrontation.

As I reached their door, however, I realized that the conversation wasn't between sisters, but between my Emma Grace and God. Emma was praying, pouring out her heart to the One who made her. Talk about feeling like a heel, misjudging a situation! Honestly, I wanted her to have her privacy, but I also didn't want to leave the moment.

It was so *compelling* to listen to a child communicate with God.

I had the feeling, *"This is how He wants me to communicate."* I leaned back against the wall, so grateful for their relationship, so grateful to God that, without me even knowing it, He was pursuing my daughter and she was responding to His gracious pursuit. It was truly an amazing moment. But then it got a bit more amazing when it struck me, *"That's not just my daughter in there. That's my sister! We share the same Father in Heaven, and the same brother—Jesus."* I'll never forget *those* goose bumps. Especially after what happened next.

When my spiritual voyeurism was just too much to bear, I left to give her her rightful privacy. I was checking my email in the bonus room when she wandered in. Playing the fool I asked, *"Hey, sweetie. Are you having trouble sleeping?"* "No," she said, *"I was just talking to God."* I smiled and probed gently, *"Do you do that often honey?"*

Her face brightened.
"Oh yeah! We talk every night."

Whew. Tears of joy streamed down my face. *"Oh Emma, I love that you do that. I talk to Him too."* She nodded and turned to walk away: *"Good night daddy."* And I just sat in awe of God. Somehow, email had no place in the richness of that moment.

Only God could've designed it this way. As if *saving* us wasn't enough, He delights to give us the gift of spiritual siblings, brothers and sisters for the journey ahead. *Some* of them happen to be blood relatives—which is sweet, but *most* of them aren't. And it doesn't even matter. Since we share the same Father, because of the same brother, Jesus, we are bound to one another through the same Spirit. So, we're not just members of a club, like Costco or the local gym—fellow-customers; we're siblings in a family. And not just *any* family, but *the* family that will last forever.

Shouldn't this *radically alter* **how we view one another?**

The writers of the New Testament certainly think so. Well over 200 times they refer to the disciples of Jesus as "brothers"—siblings. And they caught this from Jesus Himself. In Matthew 12, like He does on so many occasions, Jesus surprises His listeners. While speaking with His disciples, Jesus' mother Mary and His brothers (James is the only one we have a name for) arrive eager to speak with Him. Instead of yielding to their urgent desire, however, Jesus seizes the situation as a teachable moment. *"Who is my mother, and who are my brothers"* (Matthew 12:48)? Now, of course Jesus is not clueless as to who gave Him birth—in fact, He loved Mary very much—or who gave Him trouble in the backyard. He is making a point.

There is an *earthly* family to which you naturally or biologically belong, with which you share physical traits, last names and memories, and also geography, tradition, and tastes. And these similarities are all well and good. But there is another family to which you *can* belong and into which Jesus invites you. This family is defined, not by what you look like or where you're from, but by *who* you know, or who you've come to know. In particular, a family defined by God Himself.

Jesus points to the disciples around Him and says, *"Here are my mother and my brothers"* (Matthew 12:49). Again, He has no intention of putting His own blood relatives down; He just has every intention of elevating His own disciples to a place of relational importance they couldn't have imagined.

**A relational bond He knew
they would *need* in His absence.**

In other words, being able to trace your bloodline back to Jesus of Nazareth is of no consequence. What's critical is that you trace your *faith* back to Jesus' Father who is in Heaven. It's not about being Jewish or wealthy or educated or whatever we might imagine sets people apart as special or worthy. What matters is an *inward* growing dependence upon God's grace,

**expressing itself in an *outward*,
growing obedience to God's will.**

All the things that naturally divide us fall to the wayside as Jesus and the Holy Spirit unite us as siblings to God as our Father. You can be any age, any color, or any nationality. Your past can be relatively squeaky clean (though we all know better) or shamefully stained. The common denominator in the Family of God is a forgiven sinner's relationship with Jesus characterized by a growing desire to honor His Father's will just like Him. As Jesus concludes, *"My mother and sister and brother is anyone who does the will of My Father in heaven"* (Matthew 12:50).

And it is God's will first and foremost that you and I receive the gift of His Son.

Jesus is the doorway into *this* forever family.

It's all-*inclusive* in the sense that no one is automatically rejected, but it is totally *exclusive* in the sense that Jesus is the only way in. All roads do *not* lead to God in the same way. In John 10, as the Good Shepherd, Jesus says, *"I am the door. If anyone enters by Me, he* (or she) *will be saved and go in and out and find pasture."* (John 10:9). Or again, *"I am the way, and the truth, and the life. No one comes to the Father except through Me"* (John 14:6).

Have you received the gift of Jesus? Have you accepted the gift of being *born* into the Family of God? What keeps you from seeing other disciples as your spiritual siblings? How might you relate to them differently if you did? Now to be sure, the Christian family is huge, a global household, with millions on the reunion spreadsheet. So, you can't possibly carry on deep, meaningful relationships with *all* of your siblings (though perhaps in eternity with a finite number of siblings and an infinite amount of time…we might!). You can't even link deeply with everyone in your local church. And that is OK.

The question is:
are you linked deeply with *anyone*?

If you're a man, do you have one or two brothers, or if a woman, one or two sisters, who know you top to bottom, inside and out, your fears, your longings, and your dreams. Do you have a few you connect with intentionally, deeply, and regularly? A few with whom you can finally drop the mask and be yourself—the broken you, the restored you, the growing you, the still stubborn you? Do you have siblings? Soul companions? Sisters of the heart? A band of brothers? In order to learn to live in grace and faithfully live out the tangible love of Christ—the many "one another's" commanded in the New Testament—we must have a few close siblings with whom we can practice. Do you have them? Are you taking steps to link more deeply with a few? If not, can you identify what is holding you back? You might consider exploring these barriers with someone.

SACRIFICE

The vulgar language and intense violence notwithstanding, the movie, *Lone Survivor* captures a level of deep commitment and profound sacrifice rarely encountered. As the title suggests, only one of four Navy SEALS makes it out of a special ops mission in Afghanistan alive. Were it not for the heroic passion these men had for one another, however, none of them would have made it; their story would be buried with their bodies in rock and sand.

Literally outnumbered 40 to one, this band of brothers fought valiantly. Though each had a unique function, they operated as one. Hearts pounding out of their chests due to adrenaline and fear, but beating in sync each one for the other. When one took a bullet to the shoulder or leg, the one to his left covered him with gun raised, while the one to his right nursed his wound.

They weren't so much four individuals
as *one* organism.

Each man keeping an eye on the others, always ready to drop everything for each other's well-being.

They left all impulse for self-preservation back at the base. Their reflex was for each other. They caught each other, held each other, carried each other. When one was losing hope, another would inspire. When one was losing life, another would weep with him to his final breath. And at one point, one man literally climbed a rock outcropping to obtain a satellite phone signal. Even though he knew it would require his life at the hands of sniper fire, he did it. He just did it. And were he here to explain why, he would probably point to the lone survivor and say, *"So that he could live."*

Now, I completely understand that the drama of the last three paragraphs can feel a bit over the top as I transition us back into *linking deeply with a few.* But as I watched the film, I found myself thinking of all the men God has graciously placed in my life along the journey, not only to ensure my survival, but to help me flourish. Each one was uniquely fit for each particular season.

Jesus didn't die and rise to give us just a little taste of life. He made the greatest sacrifice to give us life to the fullest. And it was *His* plan that fullness of life would come in rich community. This is why I also found myself thinking of all the present-day disciples of Jesus who are languishing in isolation, sitting ducks for the cares of the world to overwhelm them, the lure of the world to entice them, and the lingering threat of the King's enemy to tempt them into total desertion at best, but spiritual complacency at least.

And I was *grateful* and *sad* at the same time.

Do you have someone in your life watching your spiritual back, keeping a regular eye on your soul's well-being? Are you doing the same for someone else? Do you have someone in your life with whom you are learning to live out this call to uncommon sacrifice? In Philippians 2 Paul casts a dramatic vision of Christ's selfless love we are to have for one another: *"be of the same mind, have the same love, be in full accord…do nothing from rivalry or conceit, but in humility count others more significant than yourselves. Let each of you look not only to his own interests, but also to the interests of others"* (Philippians 2:2-4).

I read this and I am convicted every time. My default is to think about *me*, to want what I want, when I want it. And if there is any energy left, then I'll think of someone else. Sure, that's a bit overstated, but by and large it's honest.

Honest, **but not like the heart of Jesus.**

The love Paul describes is a love modeled for us profoundly by Jesus Himself. A love that is eager to identify and meet the needs of another, even at great cost. And I find that challenging. But I can also testify that I have tasted the sweetness of this kind of fellowship. I have received and even extended this "others-oriented" love, and it *is* worth overcoming your timidity to experience. To our own demise we convince ourselves that we are immune to the need of such love, *and* we forget that it isn't really about us anyway!

This is perhaps the greatest pitfall in most of our relationships: we tend to choose the ones that suit us best—which isn't *all* bad— but then we happily hang in there only as long as *our* needs are being met. And when they aren't, we begin to pull back. Sometimes this pull-back comes off like a wounding outburst, but more often than not it lands in the form of a silent treatment.

We create *distance.*

And the awkwardness only grows. And perhaps unawares we reveal an unhealthy dependence on this person to satisfy us. Which is like setting someone up to fail, because who can possibly meet your needs the way you long for them to? Especially when they're so needy as well? We all are.

Now, can we be a channel of grace for one another? Absolutely. In fact in Ephesians 4 Paul coaches us to speak good words aimed at building one another up *"that it may give grace to those who hear"* (Ephesians 4:29). We are to intentionally avoid being bitter or angry with each other. Instead we are to be *"kind to one another, tenderhearted, forgiving one another as God in Christ forgave you"* (Ephesians 4:32). That last phrase is the key.

We cannot *give* **what we do not** *have.*

And we cannot expect from one another what we are not willing to receive from Christ alone *"…as God in Christ forgave you."*

Think of your closest relationships for a moment. What is your true motivation in loving them? *That* is an exposing question. I invite you to allow the Spirit to meddle a little bit with your personal incentive: *"Do I love in order to get a love I don't have and long for, or do I love as the overflow of Christ's satisfying love I'm actively receiving?"*

**<center>*That* just may be one of the most
important questions you ever answer.</center>**

I know for me it is often rather mixed. But healthy relating requires that we grow to find our identity, value, and security — our personal wholeness — not in those *around* us but in the One *within* us. When that is *not* happening, we are ill-prepared to love well. When we take our eyes off Jesus and look instead to one another, we often miss the very love we desperately need, while placing a burden on a friend they can't possibly bear.

Now, does Jesus intend to love us through one another? Absolutely. Paul does say, *"be imitators of God…and walk in love"*. But then He modifies: *"as beloved children…as Christ loved us and gave Himself up for us"* (Ephesians 5:1-2). Are you growing to really believe that you are in fact the beloved of God? Are you learning to receive daily the rich, boundless love of Christ for you personally? As you learn to receive love, you will be equipped and empowered to give it away. And others can receive *from* Christ *through* you. The more this happens, there will be less lone survivors and more loved "thrivers."

ENCOURAGEMENT

USA 6:25.4, Italy 6:26.0, Germany 6:26.4. Look at the hair's difference between those numbers again. These were the final times in the greatest Olympic race of the 1936 Berlin games. It was a 2000 meter regatta held just outside Grunau, Germany. 75,000 screaming fans were on their feet, including Adolf Hitler. The Germans had basically swept all of the races up to the final one and they were neck and neck with Italy to the very end. That is, until an unknown crew of college boys from the University of Washington dug deeper within themselves than ever before.

The lead rower, Don Hume, was physically ill going into the race, so the team knew the odds were wildly against them. But with the city of Seattle deeply invested, and with the opportunity before them to defeat Hitler's oarsmen in his own water in front of the world, eight rowers reached down and found another gear. Bob Moch, the coxswain, called to them, guided them, encouraged them, and exhorted them to the finish line. After a race that took almost six-and-one-half-minutes, only one measly second separated the three boats from one another. The Huskie-boys forced Hitler to listen to the *"Star-spangled Banner"* instead of *"Deutchland Uber Alles."*

Like every other "team", a rowing team is made up of individuals with particular roles to contribute. Unlike most teams, however, one of the roles is played by a non-rower: the *coxswain*. This isn't to say he/she isn't an athlete—most are, but they are unique in the boat as they face the opposite direction of the other athletes and use their eyes, mind, and voice instead of oars. Without them, brawny rowers would veer off in unproductive and even dangerous directions. Without the rhythm of their calling, the rowers would find themselves out of sync, fighting one another's pace instead of working in synchrony. They are the strategists, the coaches on the water. They know every stage of the race down to a science. They know when and how to call for *more* effort, and when it's time to rest the muscles for the last push. They can spot the opponent and offer words of encouragement as the bodies of their exhausted teammates threaten to give up. They never even touch the water, but a wise, demanding, faithful pilot is indispensable to a boat's success.

And so it is in a *disciple's* race as well.

Do you ever find yourself overwhelmed by the details of life? Or, suddenly thrown by hard news? Or, just worn out and in need of rest and recharge? Are you ever tempted to pull your oar out of the water for a while and just…coast? This is all of us from time to time, because following Jesus is a daunting enterprise. It is so easy to lose sight of the goal and forget the plan. In a blink, we can find ourselves "off course," vulnerable to the enemy and just spinning our paddles fruitlessly. It doesn't mean we're bad disciples, or that we're deserting the truth; nor does it mean our profession of faith is misleading or disingenuous. A fair amount of "rowers" are tired and are simply unclear as to the way forward in the Christian life. And often that's because they don't have a coxswain facing them, looking them in the eye, helping them move forward into greater faithfulness.

Whether we want to admit it or not,
we *need* that.

May I be so bold as to say that you need to be linked deeply with a few: a comrade or two who can call you out, pick you up, affirm your effort, yet call for more than you thought possible? You need people who really know you—how you're wired, where you're vulnerable—so they can remind you of the timely importance of rest, can extend to you the critical gift of grace, and encourage you to press on when the going gets tough. 'Cause it does. And they can believe, when you struggle to believe. They can pray *for* you and they can pray *with* you. They can rejoice in your victories and weep in your defeats. They can't live your life for you, just like a coxswain doesn't row, but they're simply indispensable for spiritual vitality. We're just not made to row blindly.

Now, invariably the questions arise: who are these "courageous encouragers"—spiritual coxswains? Do they exist? How do you get one? How do you keep one? Well, we're all different and there isn't a magic potion you can drink, an app you can download, or a sign-up sheet you can autograph. These kind of deep, meaningful relationships take time to develop, and you may very well strike out a few times along the way. It happens, and the discouragement can make you gun-shy from ever trying again. But don't mislead yourself into thinking you can live without it.

**Nothing makes you more vulnerable in life
as choosing to go it *alone*.**

And remember, like our previous theme, it isn't just about *you*!

This gift of deep knowing and exhorting is a gift we *give* as much as *receive*. The kind of "link" relationship I'm describing has a *mutuality* built into its DNA. Not only do you need someone to spot and spur you on to *love* God, *honor* Jesus, and *follow* the Holy Spirit, but they need you as well. We're all to play two roles in the boat, not just one. We're rowers in our own lives, and coxswains in each other's. And when *that* is in place, look out! Growth, maturity, faithfulness, fruitfulness, life...etc. Abundant life.

So how do you begin? Well, without being uncomfortably presumptuous (and you'll probably know it when you are), perhaps the first step is simply asking God to lead you to someone *you* might encourage. You don't start by barking at them to dig deep (though you may get there in time). You start by acknowledging how you see Jesus in them, and how Jesus in them spurs you on to want more of Jesus in you. And you pray. And you invite God to lead you into *link*.

And, you learn the art of listening, both to God and to others. Coxswains are champion listeners. They listen to the boat on the water, listen to the strength of the rowers' breathing, and listen to the rhythm of the oars cutting the lake, while at the same time listening to the wind and its direction.

Always **listening.**

And then responding. One of the greatest gifts we can give each other inside the family of God is tuning our ears to one another. I have found that good listening is contagious and attractive. Who has God placed in your life that you can encourage? Like a coxswain, the writer of Hebrews calls out, *"Let's consider how to stir up one another to love and good works, not neglecting to meet together, as is the habit of some, but encouraging one another, and all the more as you see the Day drawing near"* (Hebrews 10:24-25). Like the finish line of faith, the Day is drawing near. My day. Your day. His day. God has given us to each other to help one another get there. Who might you help...get there?

VULNERABILITY

Most of us have a great longing to be accepted by others. This is all the more true during the teenage years. At least it was for me. And as a rather scrawny, pale skinned, freckled, red-headed Christian this felt like an uphill climb in a large public school environment. Thankfully I had a skill: I was a pretty good golfer. And as a freshman I made varsity, which meant that right out of the gate in the fall I had a place, an identity. Not that the golf team was popular with the really cute girls in school, but I had an "in" with some upperclassmen, which was pretty cool. What I didn't realize was my misplaced "need" for acceptance would set me up to make an unfortunate decision that would dog me for years.

It was a few matches into the season and I was given the privilege of playing fifth man, which meant my round of golf counted. I knew it was very possible that we would be tied two and two coming down to my personal match. Mano-a-mano. The weight of the moment mounted as the match played out. I desperately wanted Coach and the other guys to be pleased with me. (Isn't it amazing how much of life is spent trying to impress others?) And when our longings, which are often very normal, get misplaced, we're tempted to adjust our ethics, or suspend them altogether. *"What can it really hurt?"*

Self-justification **began to set in.**

I hit a pitching wedge and my Titleist flew over the green, the backside of which was long, untrimmed grass. Though I knew it was there somewhere, I couldn't find my ball. My heart started pounding, sweat came to my brow. *"I can't afford a penalty stroke!"* And then it occurred to me, *"You don't really deserve a penalty stroke.*

This grass should have been cut. Some loser groundskeeper isn't doing his job. How is that my fault? And…if this was a legitimate tournament there would be an official spotter with our group. Surely, he would've seen where it went." I began to rationalize. Do you ever do that? It's what makes "temptation" so *tempting.*

"I had better do it fast," I thought, as my opponent was walking up to the green. *"This is just. This is fair. I'm not doing anything wrong. I'm setting right a wrong!"*

Oh, the *deceitfulness* of sin.

And then the nail in the coffin: *"No one will ever know!"* Incredible relief washed over me. *"Right. My little secret. And it's justified to boot."* So I released the Titleist in my hand down the side of my leg out of view. *"Found it!"* I announced. And I drank a shot of instant-satisfaction mixed with hidden shame. We're not made to stomach such elixirs.

As I walked up to the last green, surrounded by coaches and athletes, the match was all square. And I had a 12-foot putt to win the whole thing. It's what you dream of when you practice endlessly in the blistering sun and high humidity of Cincinnati summers. Well, I made the putt and my team rejoiced, just as I had hoped. I joined them in their exuberance, but I felt *dead* inside.

And then the murmurings began. My opponent was adamant that he had seen me drop a ball on the fifth hole. An earthquake rumbled in my stomach. The coaches convened, and then my coach approached me. *"Stephen, I know you're from a Christian family…"* Not a good beginning. *"…I believe you're a man of integrity. I'll defend you, but you have to tell me the truth. You didn't drop a ball, did you?"* Instantly an internal war broke out between my desire for honesty *and* acceptance. If I go with honesty my conscience is clean, the shame is washed away. But I run the risk of being kicked off the team and being branded with the Scarlett Letter: *cheater*. I grew up hearing in my home: *"Kirks don't cheat!"* I even use that with my kids today. Everything in me wanted to tell the truth. Sadly, not everything. And whatever percentage didn't won the moment. *"No coach. I'd never do that."* And armed with that lie, he defended me. And with no instant replay to validate the proper charge against me, we won.

But I *lost*. **Big.**

It was a hollow van ride home, and literally for the next 2 decades (yes, I'm serious), every single time I plunked a white tee into the ground to play the game I loved, I felt the pang of guilt. I confessed the sin to Jesus many times—many, many times— trying to *feel* forgiven. Have you ever done that? And while I didn't doubt that He forgives, something was still missing. It wasn't until I found myself—a Pastor—sitting in a room with a few men who were totally safe, that it finally hit me. *"Stephen, you gotta share this. You need to own this. You're forgiven because of the Cross of Jesus, but He intends to apply His gracious forgiveness to His people, through His people."* As Jesus' little brother James exhorts us: *"Confess your sins to one another and pray for one another, that you may be healed"* (James 5:16).

I needed to be *healed*.
So, I shared.

Now, granted it doesn't seem like a "big" sin, but it was *my* sin. *My* secret. And while particular sins clearly have different consequences, all sin grieves Jesus. God graciously gave me the courage to own my sin with those men. And with a kind spirit, which Paul recommends in Galatians 6:1 — *"you who are spiritual should restore him in a spirit of gentleness"* — they listened and restored me by extending God's grace to me. Their eyes said, "Forgiven," their smiles too. Their voices spoke it over me. My ears needed to hear it. One of the men even stood and walked over and embraced me. Forgiven. I could physically feel it. And the cumulative weight of over 20 years finally fell off. Jesus had paid for it 2000 years ago, but He was alive and well applying it to my heart through this tangible, personal exchange of honesty and grace. And these few washed my feet that day as Jesus had asked His disciples to do in imitation of Him during the Last Supper in John 13. To keep each other clean.

This kind of restoration doesn't just happen with casual acquaintances. It can happen, however, when you're linked deeply with a few people who know you top to bottom. One or two individuals with whom you can finally shed the mask and be real. It takes time to build the trust, to rest in each other's confidence. And it often takes one person to break the ice. What I haven't mentioned yet, is that my freedom to expose the grime on *my* feet was born as a result of another boldly revealing the dirt on *his*. And I watched the group respond to him with compelling grace. And I knew I needed that. We all do.

When was the last time you really owned your sin *with* another and received God's grace *through* another? Or, had the humbling privilege of extending the same? It's only as we are linked deeply that we can fulfill the charge of Hebrews 3: *"Exhort one another every day, as long as it is called 'today,' that none of you may be hardened by the deceitfulness of sin"* (Hebrews 3:13). Helping each other keep short accounts with God keeps our hearts pliable to be molded as God desires. Are you linked deeply with a few? *Deeply?* So few of us really are. If we all know we are sinners saved by the grace of God alone, what keeps us from owning our "dirt" with another? Are we really experiencing the freedom Christ's Cross secured? Who has God placed in your life with whom you might be linked? In order for us to embrace the mission to which we have been called, we desperately need to be linked. We get a taste of this mission next!

"Father, Son, & Holy Spirit,

thank You for the joy of joining You today
in Your redemption of Your world.

I say 'Yes!' to Your clear call to make new disciples.

I pray for my friends that You might reach them through me
with Your Gospel grace.

May my life be compelling and all my interactions
gracious and winsome."

3

PURSUE
future Disciples

Joy – Mission – Incarnation – Winsome

INTRODUCTION

The more things change, the more things stay the same. Especially in light of the proliferation of iPods and video games, I am always stunned as a parent when my children mimic things I used to do when I was a kid. For example, recently I heard gleeful screaming on my front lawn. I went out to discover neighborhood kids playing an intense game of "Sharks & Minnows." And I just thought to myself, *"Really? That game's still around?"* They were loving it. You remember that game, right? Both ends of the yard serve as a safe zone, while the middle is the dangerous "water," where the shark lurks, ready to pounce on the minnows crossing its path. If the shark tags you, you aren't "out of the game"; you actually become a shark and join the original shark in pursing more minnows. It's almost the antithesis of that other fun, nautical-themed children's game, "Sardines." Ever play that one? Someone hides, and the goal for the rest is to find the "hider" and huddle with that person in secret until one seeker is left.

Now, both games start with one person being "it," but the similarities end there. The central purpose of the "it" person in "Sardines" is to remain huddled in safety until the end, whereas in "Sharks & Minnows," the goal is to be in pursuit of minnows, transforming them into new sharks. In "Sardines," the seeker becomes a *hider*. In "Sharks & Minnows," however, the "hiders" are sought and transformed into *pursuers*. So naturally, success in Sardines is defined by quietly outlasting the others, while in "Sharks & Minnows" it is defined by embracing your new identity and eagerly pursuing more fish.

Which game do you think the American Church *mimics* most?

I fear we have lost our way a bit and I am as much to blame as anyone. The caricature of the Church as a "holy huddle" that delights to gather with each other in hopes of outlasting the world "out there" may not be completely accurate, but if we're willing to look in the mirror, it is awfully close. This is due in part to our own personal timidity, lingering doubt, and rather strong desire to avoid offending our "neighbor." It is also due to an increasingly hostile culture that dismisses absolute truth as out of bounds and those who claim it as outcasts. As a result we, as disciples of Jesus, often talk ourselves out of pursuing fish. We are largely playing "Sardines," while we're trying to call it "Sharks & Minnows." We try to convince ourselves that if we just huddle, more will come.

They're staying *away* in droves.

Or "schools" to keep with the fish theme.

Don't you think it's time we recover our Gospel roots? Jesus is "IT"! As the Pursuer, He graciously enters this world in eager pursuit of fish that think they're minnows but are meant for more. That's us! And once He finds you with Gospel grace, you have to fight the appealing lure of hunkering down and hiding with Jesus in secret the rest of your life. That's not where He is. He's not a dead, marinated sardine cooped up in a tin can, He's a shark! Jesus is alive and alert, roaming out in open water, always looking for another *potential* shark to join His Kingdom pursuit of others: your neighbor or co-worker, or friend.

Once you receive Gospel grace,
it's like, *"Tag, you're it!"*

Once pursued, you become a pursuer of others with the same grace that found you. In other words, as disciples of Jesus we are receivers and pursuers every day for the rest of our lives! Or as Jesus Himself said to His first disciples, Peter and Andrew, *"Follow me, and I will make you fishers of men"* (Matthew 4:19). In the game "Sardines," living sardines join dead ones in silence. In "Sharks & Minnows," little exhausted minnows just trying to survive are "caught" and released to become confident pursuers with a mission, living on purpose. The world—your neighborhood, office, school, grocery store, athletic team...etc.—it is the open water. And as a disciple of Jesus, through His Spirit within you, Jesus is still *in* the world...still *in* pursuit! And you have the privilege and joy of joining His mission.

Who are those you live with or near, work with, or play with, buy from or sell to that are outside the faith, but inside your reach? Think about that.

Who is *outside* **Gospel faith,**
but *inside* **your gracious reach?**

What if you began to believe that, instead of mere random chance, God intentionally places you in the midst of others so they might experience Gospel grace through you? Are you open to that? Are you beginning to pray toward that end? Let's consider together what that might look like.

JOY

A pastor was given a unique opportunity to play a round of golf at the local Country Club. The only problem was that the offer was for Sunday. The pastor mulled it over and decided to "call in sick" and take advantage of the invitation. Sure, he felt a little guilty, as he should, but he also felt blessed to play this exclusive course. When he got to the first tee, St. Peter up in Heaven (so yes, this is a fable) questioned why God would allow this round to proceed. God knew what He was doing. The pastor teed off on the par four and God brought an extra gust of wind, blowing the drive down the fairway, onto the green and right into the hole! St. Peter was shocked and questioned again the wisdom of being so gracious to this hooky-playin' fool. To which God replied with an ornery grin, *"Who's he gonna tell?"* And of course the idea is that when you have really good news

the *ultimate* **joy is in the sharing.**

My son and I enjoyed a golf weekend in Georgia one Fall. We did actually play on Sunday. (At least I'm being honest.) We played pretty well on Sunday, but it was the Monday round that we came home telling the world about. He chipped in for birdie on the first hole, and I followed up by chipping in for birdie on the second *and* the third. It was a surreal experience! Of course it was a total blast in the moment, but again the greater joy was sharing the news with others who found it amazing.

In this lifelong priority of PURSUE, we often approach those who are outside the faith whom God has placed inside our reach—a neighbor, a friend, a co-worker—like the pastor in the initial joke. Having found this amazing good news of Gospel grace—or *having been* found—we're often and unfortunately somewhat ashamed or afraid to tell anyone about it.

**So we just keep
our hole-in-one—*Grace*—a secret.**

What would need to happen for you to shed this common embarrassment and embrace the joy of announcing with your life and your words the grace that has found you and set you free? I want to be less like the pastor that had to bite his tongue and more like the pastor who couldn't stop telling people about all the chip-in's. How 'bout you?

Think about a time in your life when you experienced something really exciting or rare and you couldn't wait to tell loved ones about it. The births of our children and the first time we saw the face of our adopted son immediately come to mind. Perhaps for you it was receiving an engagement ring, or a job offer, or the selling of a home, or the photo you took of a whale breeching off the coast of Alaska. Life is chock-full of these *Instagram* moments.

Since we tend to joyfully share good news quickly, why do you think it is so difficult for us to share the greatest news our hearts have ever heard?

It is a bit *curious*, isn't it?

Let me offer three reasons to get us thinking. The first isn't easy to admit. Some of us hesitate to share Jesus because, while we're pretty convinced ourselves, we don't personally have verifiable evidence to support the Gospel story. Sharing Christ forces you to wrestle at the deepest level with whether or not you really believe the news you're passing on. An engagement has a *ring*, a pregnancy has a *test*, a birth has a *baby*, and my son and I witnessed each other's chip-ins—evidence. Pursuing others with Gospel grace feels like a bit of a leap. *"Do I really believe?"* That's a good question worth exploring before you ask others to believe.

A second reason why sharing Christ seems "unnatural" is that most of us haven't formed friendships with those outside the faith. As we said, it's quite common for Christians to huddle like sardines, intentionally quarantined away from the world. I don't tend to tell complete strangers about my golf game. It does seem odd, then, that I would tell a mere acquaintance about a relationship I have with a Jew named Jesus who died nearly 2000 years ago, but who I believe now lives because he overcame death through a resurrection. Let's be honest;

that does seem a bit *peculiar*.

But what does that then mean? One of two things. Either gospel grace is reserved for those I know and love and so I never share with a *potential* disciple outside of my family and closest friends, or it's high time I step out of my comfort-zone and risk pursuing connection with those who don't yet know Jesus. The presence of a real growing relationship is the necessary context for sharing the greatest news of your life. When you discover common ground and take a genuine interest in what matters most to them, they will likely reciprocate. It may take time, but patience is one of grace's greatest virtues.

A third reason we may be hesitant to share Gospel grace with future disciples of Jesus is that we haven't embraced the Gospel role to which we've been called. The Gospel story includes a Christmas manger, an Easter tomb, and a glorious Return. But in the meantime, God is busy all around us pursuing men, women, and children with Gospel grace. And His primary chosen instrument is people like you and me.

Who better to *extend* grace than those of us who are *receiving* it?

The apostle Paul explains that the gift of salvation comes with a new vocation: *"we are ambassadors for Christ, God making His appeal through us"* (2 Corinthians 5:20). This means whether we make a home or a product for a living, or even if we are retired, we have a meaningful mission every minute of every day as representatives of Jesus Himself.

We are literally called to "re-present" Jesus. In the first century, He was present in the flesh; now in the twenty first century, He remains present through us, by His Spirit. When according to Paul is the *"favorable time and the day of salvation"* (2 Corinthians 6:2)? The time is NOW. Today. That means every day has eternal implications. Today God is *"reconciling the world to Himself"* and He's chosen to *"give us the ministry of reconciliation, entrusting to us*

81

the message of reconciliation" (2 Corinthians 5:18-19). It is common for presidents and kings to send envoys or emissaries to foreign lands on their behalf to promote policy or communicate important news. These ambassadors maintain their uniqueness, but they don't speak on their own. Rather, what they say, and how they act is a direct reflection on the one who sent them.

So it is with *us.*

This old, broken world is foreign territory for Gospel grace. And most of the people who live here don't know the One who made them, nor the One who's willing to save them. That's why we're here. We've been sent on a mission into our neighborhoods and schools, grocery stores, offices and ballfields to champion grace on behalf of the One who offers it freely. Our lives are not to be obstacles that keep people from receiving grace—either because we're unkind in our engagements or disengaged altogether; they are to be clear windows through which the grace of King Jesus shines brightly. Our pursuit of others, not as projects in need of a moral fix but as people in need of genuine love, is how God is reconciling the world to Himself. In our words and actions, through our lives *"God is making His appeal through us"* (2 Corinthians 5:20).

Do you think those outside the faith find God *appealing* through you?

And are you beginning to discover the joyful wonder of participating in God's redemption of His world? That, in addition to including us in His *family*, God graciously includes us in His *mission*? We're made for this! The King's Cross is the sole source of salvation, and we are ambassadors of this saving King. Which is quite a title, and quite an assignment. Are you willing to ask God daily to equip you for it, to find increasing joy in it? He is eager to make it so!

Oh and by the way, in case you were wondering, on the fourth hole my son and I both hit two balls out of bounds. Ha! God has a way of keeping us humble, doesn't He?

MISSION

Did you ever play "Capture the Flag" as a kid? Two teams are given a territory divided by a "safe zone" where both teams can roam without being caught. The goal is to protect *your* hidden flag and to *find* theirs, returning it to your side without being touched by an opposing player. It was my most favorite game growing up. And one crisp autumn evening when I was in high school I found myself in enemy territory. Leaning back against a tree, I saw the enemy's flag just two feet above my head in all of its glory! This was my moment.

I quietly grabbed the flag and began to plot my way back to the safe-zone, to victory. All of a sudden I heard the voices of two girls. I think they were just talking about make-up or something. Then an adult leader joined them, and then some of my buddies started coming and my heart started thumping. Here I sat with their prized jewel in my hand. They would so want to *get* me. The voices drew too close for comfort so I counted to three and bolted.

Immediately, the gig was up. I ran as fast as I could, bursting through tree limbs, branches and bushes, numbed by the rush of the moment. *"Just get to the safe zone,"* I thought. The chase would end and I'd bask in the glory of my catch. But they were hot on my heels: *"Get Kirk! Get Kirk!"* Someone came from my left and then my right. I got confused and began to panic. Thankfully, I heard *my* teammates cheering for me from the right. They fueled my blitz.

I looked over my shoulder and saw my best friend only a few yards off. I turned back around only to run straight through a huge thorn bush. Scrapes everywhere. I'm screaming, he's screaming, but we were full speed ahead, I for my life, he for his flag. My legs were on fire, my heart was pumpin' out of my chest. 50 yards. 40. 30. I broke through the edge of the wood and the safe zone was right before me. It was a sprint to the finish. I was the hero!

And then...*everything* changed.

With my attention riveted on the safe zone before me and *Mr. Wheels* himself behind me, I never saw sweet little Allison. A shy girl, who until that moment had just been contentedly sitting in the safe-zone longing for this dreadful, boring event to come to an end. It felt like slow motion. She saw me, stood up, crossed the line toward me, and just tapped me on the shoulder as I dived past. Eric and I lay in a heap, gasping for air. Allison came over, took the flag that was almost glued to my hand and said, *"Get up Stephen. I get to take you to jail!"* Just a few feet from a victory that was not meant to be.

Now, what does *this* have to do with
our pursuit of future disciples?

I think there are a number of important parallels. Our pursuit of people with Gospel grace has an inherent quality to it: *motion.* Movement. And unlike centripetal force which is inward movement—literally, *pedaling towards the center*—Gospel pursuit is centrifugal in its outward direction—literally, *fleeing from the center*. In fact, the very last words of Jesus recorded in Matthew 28 illustrate this. They have become known as the Great Commission, but they could just as rightly be called the Great Go-mission, because in Jesus' departure He authorizes His disciples to move out in His name making *new* disciples of all nations through baptism and discipleship (Matthew 28:19-20). Leading people *to* Jesus and growing them *in* Jesus. With the same tenacity that I pursued my territory and the singular focus with which Eric pursued me, so we are to pursue those around us who do not yet know just how much they matter to God. Head up, eyes open, hearts pounding with a growing passion for people.

What keeps you from initiating
this *chase* of grace?

It is the clear call of a disciple to pattern our lives after the One we follow. It is not optional extra credit for the really committed disciple; it is fundamental for *all* disciples. As Jesus said after His resurrection, *"As the Father has sent me, even so I am sending you"* (John 20:21). *That* is how it works. Remember from Sharks and Minnows: *"Tag, you're it!"* Jesus arrives in pursuit of a small band of everyday, ordinary people: fishermen, tax-collectors, homemakers, prostitutes—sinners. And then He entrusts them with His on-going mission in His world. Just like Jesus, we are to be seeking out and folding in those who do not yet know Him. Think of the eagerness of those first disciples. The moment he discovers Jesus, we see Andrew running to get his brother Peter— *"We have found the Messiah!"* (John 1:41). Likewise, Philip stopped at nothing to tell his brother Nathanael: *"We have found...Jesus of Nazareth"* (John 1:45). Or in John 4:1-45, Jesus breaks all Jewish social taboo by deliberately pursuing an outcast of outcasts. She was an *adulteress,* she was a *Samaritan,* and she was a *woman.* Surely, He would steer clear of her.

Yet Jesus considered her *worth* it.

He eagerly pursued, taking a genuine interest in her as a person, delighting to offer her life. And what was her response? She mirrored her Savior. She pursued. *"She left her water jar* (at the well) *and went away into town"* inviting everyone within earshot to meet Jesus (John 4:28-29). Do you not want that same enthusiasm to grow in you?

It wasn't present in Allison. Remember the girl who *ruined* the Capture the Flag game. Don't worry I don't harbor ill will. Ha! But her contented disengagement, waiting the game out in the safety of the middle-zone, *is* a common unhealthy approach for many disciples of Jesus. The lure of remaining in our comfort-zones, minding our own business, biding our time in secret or private devotion is strong for all of us. Self-justification rises with such ease:

But I'm an introvert.
I'm too busy.
It will take too much energy.
What if I fail?
I don't even like this game—evangelism.
Others will take care of it.
Others are better at this than me.
What difference can I make anyway?

And I'm pretty sure there are many more. I have plenty of my own reasons why I want to avoid this clarion call to pursue future disciples. But it's not as optional as Allison made it look.

Which brings us to a second parallel to the "game": *participation*. Somehow, someway, each of us needs to discover the role Jesus intends for us to play in His pursuit of His world. For most, that will not mean cross-culture mission, though in melting-pot America is there any other kind? God has wisely placed the nations in our own back yard! Some may be called to church plant in Tokyo or to provide orphan care in Guatemala, but for most of us our pursuit is going to happen right where we are, right where we live: with neighbors, co-workers, family, and friends. Maybe it will be the woman at the checkout, your mechanic or hairstylist, or maybe your child's teacher. Think of the people you cross paths with every week, every day. In a culture where it is increasingly common to don the "happy face" and to settle for superficial relating through social media,

people are *starved* for genuine pursuit.

They may not be able to articulate it, but the longing for the grace we know is strong within them. Comfortable Allison eventually stood up and courageously played her role. What will it take for you to do the same?

It may take the third and final parallel to the game: *encouragement*. I remember feeling exhausted and disoriented as I ran through the woods. It wasn't until I heard the cheers of my own teammates that I rediscovered my sense of direction. They got me back on track and their enthusiasm fueled my pursuit of the goal. God has graciously given us to one another in order to help us stay focused on the mission. Do you have a few people who are keeping you focused? Who has God uniquely placed within your reach that happens to be outside the faith? Are you praying for them, for God's Spirit to be wooing them? Are you praying for yourself, that you might be open, creative, and faithful in your pursuit? Thankfully, it's not up to us to save anyone. That's God's work. But Jesus *has* chosen to do much of His saving work through His disciples. Are you willing to get in the game?

INCARNATION

True confession: I often think *I* know best. Sadly, this is even true when I don't have much expertise. One such occasion happened during our adoption training as we were preparing to welcome a new life from a foreign land into our hearts. Of course, what do *I* know about international adoption? And yet, one afternoon I managed to challenge our social worker as if I knew best.

She was recommending that we learn as much about Ethiopia as possible and that we celebrate Ethiopian culture *visually* in our home. That made a great deal of sense to me, but I began to wonder internally about the wisdom of making our new son feel so radically "different." I wanted him to know that he was as fully one of our children as any of his six siblings. But I wisely kept my thoughts to myself. That is, *until* the social worker suggested that we even celebrate particular Ethiopian holidays throughout the year. I began to protest: *"Don't you think overemphasizing his Ethiopian heritage inadvertently reinforces that he doesn't really belong here?"* Boom! I actually thought I had made an observation this social worker had never considered. Maybe I just helped advance her in *her* training! I'm incorrigible. Just ask my wife.

Her response blew me away. *"Stephen, in your zeal to make him American, you're forgetting that by adopting him you are becoming*

Ethiopian. The pictures on your walls and your new celebrations are as much a reminder for you as they are for him." Ouch! Checkmate. It was one of those moments of cerebral and cardiac clarity that I will never forget. In my effort to fold him into our world, I was forgetting to enter fully into his. Nothing could possibly create a stronger bridge across which his heart could eventually walk into ours, than our willingness to incarnate into the world he was being asked to leave behind. The only world he'd ever known. How could I ask a seven-month-old to adapt if I was not willing to lead the way? The onus of *accommodation* was on me, and that insight radically impacted how we celebrate Ethiopia with our son.

Might a similar shift be *necessary* as we pursue those outside the faith?

Are they not coming from "foreign" territory too? Most churches are willing to have the "lost" stumble in as long as they adopt new ways. But perhaps we ought to bear the greater burden in building the bridge? After all, they're the ones who have so much to lose, leaving behind all they've ever known for a new, unfamiliar experience. Supposedly, as disciples of Jesus we've already lost our lives and gained the riches of Christ. So, are we not free? Having been delivered from the captivity of self-concern and self-promotion should we not eagerly incarnate into *their* world, meet them on *their* turf, adapt to *their* ways, even adopt some of *their* language, and traditions, and practices? We're willing to have them walk across the bridge into our world, but in lieu of a bridge, who's willing to build one that reaches into theirs?

Jesus was *willing*.

His incarnation declares in neon lights the audaciously bold willingness of God to condescend. God's Son *divested* Himself of the familiarity of Heaven in order to *invest* Himself in the lives of those who were spurning the very Glory He humbly relinquished. Amazing! The richest One impoverished Himself in order to enrich the poor. *That's* unrivaled sacrifice. That's mind-bending, gracious accommodation. And apparently it caught on.

The apostle Paul incorporated this incarnational strategy into his own personal mission, making the truth and grace of the Gospel accessible to as many as possible. He champions this unexpected missional accommodation: *"Though I am free from all, I have made myself a servant to all, that I might win more of them…I have become all things to all people that by all means I might save some"* (1 Corinthians 9:19,22). In other words, Paul was so free in Christ virtually nothing hindered him from drawing near to those who needed Gospel grace. Prior to meeting Christ, Paul was bound to one set of exclusive traditions—an old dog stubbornly disinclined to new tricks. But having received Gospel grace, Jesus set him free to lovingly participate in all kinds of cultural experiences with a whole cast of "unsightly" characters he might otherwise have avoided.

Have you read the four Gospel accounts at the beginning of the New Testament? Learn from Jesus Himself as He models a life of freedom and missional adaptation: eating food, enjoying drinks (even providing really good ones!); attending parties, befriending and, yes, even defending sinners with courageous joy *and* without fear of Gospel compromise. Far from huddling in quarantine, Jesus initiated everyday interactions with a commitment to remove any obstacles to grace the so-called "religious" had constructed—some intentionally, some inadvertently.

What *obstacles* have we placed
in the way of future disciples of Jesus?

Perhaps you find yourself questioning Paul's cavalier style, seeing it as a slippery slope into sin and concession. But surely Paul, like Jesus before him, stopped short of involving Himself in immoral practices that Jesus condemned. Contextualizing the Gospel is not an unthinking promotion of sin, but a genuine pursuit of sinners. In our effort to avoid condoning their choices and lifestyle, perhaps we've forfeited the opportunity to show them acceptance, treating them with the respect creatures made in God's glorious image deserve. The truth is, we all tend to drift to one of two unhelpful extremes. Some of us err on the *loose* side of being so compromised by the culture that we offer little contrast and thus mute our influence. Others of us err on the *legalistic* side of being so alien and disconnected from the culture that we offer little to no connection and thus similarly no chance at Gospel influence. Let's face it,

neither *pure* indulgence
nor *pure* separation is
pure Gospel.

Toward which pole do you find yourself pulled? This is what we must discern in a post-modern, increasingly post-Christian society. Some of us need to be freer to *participate* in common cultural practices that might actually open doors to future disciples, whereas others of us need to *abstain* from certain practices that keep future disciples from even knowing there's a door. A door to something new! Discerning your own personal tendency will be a huge step in making PURSUE a growing priority. Jesus' dogged determination to spend time with and to share covenantal meals with the notable, immoral rejects of society, sets the tone for those of us who follow Him. As Jesus says, *"A servant is not greater than His master"* (John 13:16). In other words, if King Jesus—the purest of the pure—is willing to place Himself in uncomfortable situations for the sake of someone tasting embodied grace, then so should we.

And that's the key—*"for the sake of...."* Paul's missional accommodation is far from flippant or aimless; he *"does it all for the sake of the Gospel, that I may share with them in its blessings"* (1 Corinthians 9:23). Rather than sitting back on his high horse demanding that pagans clean themselves up before contact, Paul initiates contact with Jews, Gentile-turned-Jews, common pagans, and the weakest around him in hopes of helping them enjoy the freedom of grace anchoring his heart.

Are you as *eager* and *willing*?

Those who regularly cross your path have a story, a formed narrative or worldview, and a particular lifestyle. Inevitably, in order to engage, you will need to cede some of your particular likes and dislikes for the greater purpose of pursuing them. But that's the journey we're on. Sobering but true, following Jesus is centrally a discovery that life isn't as much about you as you thought it was. This lifelong priority of PURSUE makes that about as clear as any of the other eight priorities. Other-worldly love motivated Jesus to leave His settled comfort-zone and enter the muck and mire of broken earth. This same love saved Paul, compelling him to do the same. Was it their preference? Not necessarily. But they showed *deference*, yielding personal preference to the greater goal of spreading the blessing of Gospel grace. Does such accommodating love compel you? If not, can you identify why? Even if you're not sure all that it will mean, are you at least willing to ask King Jesus to lead you into incarnational living? The graced are indeed the best and *only* conduits of grace. Let's explore next what this might look like in practice.

WINSOME

When I was 10-years-old my dad began discipling me in the game of golf and unconsciously in PURSUE at the same time. On the second tee dad would often build a bridge toward our playing partners: *"So, when you're not playin' golf, what do you find yourself doing?"* He was modeling for me a way of relating that demonstrates the intrinsic value of every human life *and* the value of time. People matter. And moments aren't random.

I caught that.

No one was beneath or outside my dad's pursuit. The strangers were often noticeably uncomfortable at first, but dad wasn't selling anything, he was just taking an interest in their story. If your ball needed cleaning, he'd offer to clean it. If you lost a ball, he'd walk clear out of his way to help you find it. And when you hit a good shot—even if it was just good for you—he'd make you feel like you were Jack Nicklaus. As far as I can tell, dad never led anyone in the *Sinner's Prayer* on a golf course, but I'm pretty sure he led quite a few of them a step closer to Christ than when they arrived at the club. So often Christians are known for being pushy, preachy, and opinionated. So, we actually serve the Gospel and King Jesus when we intentionally challenge these stereotypes by interacting with grace and kindness, asking questions that draw others out rather than shut them down. The Mill Course in Cincinnati is where my dad taught me how to play the game I love *and* how to love the strangers that play the game.

In Colossians 4:3 Paul coaches us to pray that God would open a door for the Word, to share Christ. I am growing to pray for that on a daily basis. Are you? Prayer reminds me of two things: *opportunities* and *dependency* upon God. There are openings to pursue future disciples all around me — waiting for me to jump in. And in order for me to be Gospel-effective I'm dependent upon God preparing the way. He prepares future disciples with whom I engage and He prepares me to engage *well*. Paul's counsel on what "well" looks like is incredibly relevant for our American context:

steward **every interaction.**

In the Greek language there are two types of "time." The one we're most familiar with is *chronos,* linear, clock time — seconds, minutes, hours, and days...etc. We live in chronos. But then there is *kairos,* which is an appointed moment in the midst of chronos that has greater weight or significance. Chronos is ordinary time, for example, 11:14 a.m. on any ordinary day. But then there's kairos — a sudden in-breaking that transforms a normal time of day or night into the extraordinary. It can be sweet and it can be hard, but kairos has arrived. It's a set-apart, "holy" moment to be processed and treasured.

Sometimes we *plan* **for kairos and sometimes we step into it** *unexpectedly.*

This is important because when Paul coaches us to be wise as we walk among those outside the faith, he clarifies by saying *"make the best use of the time"* (Colossians 4:5). And the word he chooses for "time" is kairos because Paul believes that God is always busy around us; if we are wise and aware, tuned in and open to the leading of His Spirit, ordinary moments can become eternity-shaping God-moments in an instant. Kairos.

So what does *"making the most"* look like in real life?

Well, it involves *always* taking the lead on speaking to others with grace, salting our conversations so they are tasty and appealing. Your warmth toward outsiders, created in large measure by the *manner* in which you demonstrate their value, ought to leave them wanting more, not less. This is precisely what we see in the life of Jesus. The "religious" could hardly tolerate Him, but future disciples couldn't get enough. Even many who didn't eventually sign on to be His disciples followed Him all around because of His intriguing magnetism. Are your neighbors, co-workers, and acquaintances "drawn" to you? Are they inviting you further in, or holding you at arm's length? Cultivating the character of Jesus can make all the difference.

Let me briefly offer 12 compelling characteristics of Jesus you might begin to pray for and incorporate into your pursuit of others.

HUMILITY

In a dog-eat-dog world of competition and achievement—where the end supposedly justifies the means—a humble attitude is compelling. In your interactions, are you promoting yourself or deliberately downplaying your achievements so that you can lift someone else up? A great practice on this is to ask someone for help. In John 4:7, Jesus asks the woman at the well for a drink and it changes her life. When we ask a neighbor to hold a ladder or a co-worker for an insight on a project, we demonstrate that we are not self-sufficient and we draw them in.

INITIATIVE

In a world of self-promotion where it is common to enter a room verbally or non-verbally announcing *"Here I am!"* it is compelling to arrive with a posture that communicates, *"There you are."* Note the next time you arrive at the office or school, who is taking the lead to initiate engagement? Are you trying to be noticed, or are you noticing? Since you already know that you're significant to Jesus, you're free to help someone else discover the same. That often starts with being noticed.

GENTLENESS

In a world of harsh critique and self-defense where most of us walk around with bullet-proof armored plating ready to ward off attacks and justify our behavior, it is compelling to treat people with gentleness. This is not a simple task, especially when attacked, but it is Gospel peculiar to be so settled in Christ that you are able to turn aside wrath or anger by entrusting yourself to the One who judges justly. The next time you are improperly confronted, pause long enough to remind yourself who you are and turn away wrath with a surprisingly gentle response.

THOUGHTFULNESS

In a world so often motivated by self-concern, initiating unexpected kindness is compelling. We can't give what we don't have, but if we are growing in our satisfaction in Jesus, we can give radically and meaningfully out of the overflow of His love. Sometimes we play "Secret-Santa" during December. What if you incorporated a version of that all throughout the year? "Secret-

Jesus!" Come up with a list of people you might bless with "just because" gifts. Thoughtfulness is Gospel peculiar.

FAITH

In a world filled with ache and a therapeutic culture eager to avoid or eliminate pain at all costs, it is compelling when disciples of Jesus approach hardship with growing confidence in God. Real inner peace and hope, even joy, are fascinating. You can't produce this on your own, but, as you grow daily in your faith, you prepare yourself to offer those around you a compelling picture of uncommon devotion. Our calm in the midst of the storms of life causes future disciples to wonder about the source of our anchor.

FAITHFULNESS

In a world of disposable relationships—marriages in particular—faithful, growing, fun-loving marriages that are honest about struggles but hopeful about deepening love are compelling. If you are married, any investment you make in helping your marriage flourish is actually an investment in PURSUE. As Paul explains in Ephesians 5:31-32, godly marriages illustrate to a watching world Christ's love for His disciples and our honoring response.

HELPFULNESS

In an independent world rigorously committed to being self-sufficient and sadly often self-consumed it is compelling when you go out of your way to identify real needs around you and play your part in alleviating them. Perhaps a co-worker could use your assistance on a presentation or a neighbor with their yard? You might ask your waiter/waitress if there's anything, for which you might pray. You could support a child through *Compassion* or *World*

97

Vision, or make meals and pass them out downtown. You could "adopt" a refugee family, helping them navigate life in a foreign place. Opportunities abound. Are you aware? Are you available?

LISTENING

In a world that is quick to speak and slow to listen, it is compelling whenever a person quiets themselves long enough to be present to, and mindful of, someone else. People often have a list they are working through, an agenda they are implementing, or a point they intend to make. So, they have little to no time for meaningful conversation; certainly not conversation that is steered by someone else. Are you getting equipped with listening skills and taking the time to show interest, leaning in and asking questions that draw others out?

AUTHENTICITY

In a Botox world, where people are often scheming to beat the system and lying to maintain reputation, it is compelling when you own up to places where you fall short in your day-to-day life and relationships. If you come off as plastic, always grinning from ear to ear as if everything is always hunky-dory, you actually reinforce the world's stereotype of Christians: that we are so heavenly minded we are no earthly good. We *are* aliens in the sense that we are new creatures in Christ, but we still live, move and have our being on this real, fallen sphere where life is full of challenge and disappointment. It's OK to acknowledge this as it actually points listeners to the One who *will make* all things new.

HOSPITALITY

In a world of subdivisions and cul-de-sacs, where garage-doors enable us to come and go without any neighborly interaction, it is compelling to invite those outside the faith into your home, into your life. The invitation shows interest, but then cleaning your home, preparing a meal, setting a place at *your* table reserved for *them* shows value. We all need to eat. And Jesus often seized upon this very ordinary, innocuous daily occurrence to Pursue. And frankly, this plays in both directions. It certainly did with Jesus in the Gospels. He was "guest" far more often than "host." The next time you are invited to a party or a dinner, take a risk and accept the invitation. Even if, perhaps especially if, you know the hosts have a completely different view of life than you do. Are you being invited into the homes of those outside the faith? *That* is a thought-provoking question. If so, it might be a sign that a pursuing heart is being born in you.

TIME

I suppose this goes without saying, but in a fast-paced, frenetic world that, due to technology, is always "on," having time to linger in a moment with someone outside the faith becomes a compelling opportunity. It often feels like an interruption, but might it just be *kairos*?

LIGHT

In a largely dark, cold, sad, lost, and frightened world, it is compelling when disciples of Jesus shine the light of the Gospel. Of course, if we're not mindful in *how* we shine, we can ironically blind those who see us. If we're prepared, however, deliberate and thoughtful in our every interaction, we can *illuminate* truth, *bring* warmth, *radiate* joy, *offer* direction, and *proclaim* hope for the great blessing of those who hear.

The same grace that *saves* **us**
transforms **us.**

As these characteristics of Jesus are born in you by the Holy Spirit, those who are outside the faith, whom God is placing inside your reach, will be eager to know about the source. You will be granted many opportunities to share the *"reason for the hope within you"* (1 Peter 3:15). Far from forcing the issue, God-honoring pursuit opens doors naturally in a supernatural way. As you walk through them with Gospel grace in heart and hand, you will participate in God's glorious redemption of His world. What a joy! And nothing will prepare you more for this life of mission than growing stronger in your personal relationship with God, learning to love Him as your very own Father. To this we turn next.

LOVE
God as Father

HONOR
Jesus as King

FOLLOW
the Holy Spirit

"Father, thank You for adopting me as Your son/daughter into Your forever family.

I am overwhelmed by Your abundant, tangible goodness.

I bring my needs and longings before You, trusting Your gracious supply.

I want to love You today with all of my heart, soul, and mind."

4

LOVE

God as Father

Adoption – Provision – Petition – Devotion

INTRODUCTION

Memories. Isn't it interesting that God gave us the capacity to *remember*? We are so used to the concept that we cannot imagine life without memories. Of course we do forget many former happenings as little consequence, and some recollections we wish we *could* forget because of the ache. Part of what makes life meaningful, however, is living in the *present* with the context of the *past* in mind. God came up with that idea and built it into the human experience.

I will never forget Christmas Eve, 1996. At exactly 6:00 p.m. and 15 seconds—my father-in-law took a picture of the wall clock—my life changed forever. I had already been a son, a brother, a friend, and a husband, but I had never been a *father*. Yet with a doctor's brief announcement and one clear cry, my wife and I welcomed a son into the world. I remember holding him for the first time and wondering why I was so blessed to be his dad. And also wondering if I had what it took to do it well. All of a sudden a sense of delightful duty came over me. Could I protect him, teach him, train him, and provide for him? I had no doubt of my own affection for him—that was overflowing—but I did wonder if he would know it and rest in it, and respond by loving me in return. Nineteen years later, by God's grace, he does.

My experience that snowy winter's night parallels God's relationship with everyone who receives Gospel grace. In multiple places our conversion is described as a "new birth." The Greek can mean either "born *again*" or "born *from above*" and both are probably spot on. We all have a particular date embossed on personal legal documents which declares the precise timing of our initial, earthly physical birth. In other words, we are all born once and born from below—down here. This is the date we learn to celebrate with cake and candles. And while there's certainly nothing wrong with this cultural tradition, sadly, when we were born, we were born into a broken world fractured by sin. Since our own hearts are inclined toward self and away from God from the outset, a new, second birth—a spiritual birth—becomes essential.

This is precisely what Jesus explains to a revered Jewish official named Nicodemus in John 3. Being a Jew, Nicodemus naturally presumed upon his pedigree, yet Jesus explains, *"Truly, truly* (incontrovertibly certain), *I say to you, unless one is born again* (or from above) *he cannot see the Kingdom of God"* (John 3:3). In other words, no one inherently has a sufficient pedigree. New birth is necessary, and new birth hinges

on one's *response* **to Jesus—the only true Son.**

As John explains earlier, *"...to all who did receive Him (Jesus), who believed in His name, He gave the right to become children of God, who were born, not of blood nor the will of the flesh nor of the will of man, but of God"* (John 1:12-13). Receiving Gospel grace is not merely a mental approval to new facts about God; it is a second "delivery" where you are born into His forever family. While other metaphors are employed, the primary way of understanding your new fellowship with God is one of child to parent. And in particular, child to Father. But let's step back a moment.

According to the Bible, God has *always* existed. In other words, dirt and trees, fish and bees, the Atlantic and the Arctic all came into being at a particular time. God created them in *His* time and according to *His* design. Therefore unlike creation, God is uncreated. He has always been.

There has never been a moment *without* **God.**

And interestingly, before God was Creator or Redeemer, Ruler or Judge...etc., God was Father. God has *always* been a Father to a Son. Therefore, the loving Fatherhood of God is as eternally fundamental to His being and experience as anything else.

Now, a central distinctive claim of Christianity is that, while there is only *one* God, this God has always existed in *three* distinct persons and has been revealed in redemptive history as Father, Son, and Holy Spirit. Though not appearing in Scripture as a word, this theological concept, which permeates the New Testament, is traditionally called the *Trinity*. The word "trinity" is the combination of the prefix *tri*—meaning "three," and *unity*—meaning "one." Far from suggesting that God is three competing "gods," or one God morphing into three different beings at different times and places, the New Testament affirms that God is always three persons and always completely united as one. Each— Father, Son, and Holy Spirit—has a unique role to play,

yet all three share 100%
substantive **equality and divine perspective.**

In other words, *none* of the three is more valuable than the other two—each is completely *full* of Glory. There is never even a hint of disagreement between them, always operating with one heart and mind. Always.

Admittedly the Trinity is not an easy concept to grasp. Frankly, it baffles and confounds everyone who intersects with it. But perhaps its profound mystery offers you extra incentive to press in and seek to know this unknowable, knowable God? Historically, for most of humanity, our incapacity to figure Him out completely breaks in one of two directions. Some determine that He is too foreign and enigmatic to be anything more than an immaterial myth (a figment of our imagination) and therefore disregard Him. Others humbly concede that our inability to fully comprehend Him indicates that He must be more than man-made. And if so, He is worthy of our intentional engagement at least, and perhaps even our worship as well. The blue STRONGER TRIANGLE is a reminder to us that God intends for us to get to know Him personally as Father, Son, and Holy Spirit. To the degree that we neglect any one of them, we inadvertently neglect God Himself. When you say yes to Gospel grace, you are welcomed into a relationship that has always been, a relationship of love that begins with knowing God as Father. Let's explore Him together.

ADOPTION

It is always a bit humorous to watch my young children try to piece together why certain friends look "just like" their mom or dad. Unaware of the science of genetics, they're just *amazed* at how the hair curls the same, or how the smile brightens the same, or how similar the cadence or tone of voice is. Of course in time they understand. It's almost a relief, like when the magician reveals how he does the trick, or when the mystery is solved in the end. *"Like father, like son. Like mother, like daughter,"* we say. There *is* a reason why we are often so similar. Similar tastes, looks, and personalities don't just *happen* by accident; they're created and groomed through nature and nurture. We can often spot family traits and traditions because the adage is essentially true: *"the apple doesn't fall too far from the tree."*

This is all the more true when it comes to God the Father's relationship with God the Son. God the Son, who entered human history in the first century as the Jewish man Jesus, has always been in constant, uninterrupted fellowship with God the Father. And as the *only* Son and being *fully* God, the entirety of the Father's character is perfectly mirrored in the life of the Son. As Paul says, *"For in Him* (Jesus) *all the fullness of God was pleased to dwell"* (Colossians 1:19). Or again we learn in Hebrews: *"He (Jesus) is the radiance of the glory of God and the exact imprint of His nature"* (Hebrews 1:3). The point is, if we could see and experience Jesus — which we can on the pages of the four Gospels of the New Testament (Matthew, Mark, Luke, & John) — we would experience the Father. *"No one has ever seen God; the only God, who is at the Father's side, He* (Jesus) *has made Him known"* (John 1:18) Or as Jesus Himself explains to an inquiring disciple named Philip, who simply wanted to see the Father: *"Whoever has seen me has seen the Father...I am in the Father and the Father is in me"* (John 14:9-10). In other words, in Jesus' case the apple is not only *close* to the tree, the apple and the tree are one! Jesus is the exact replica, the perfect representation of His Father in the flesh. He is, in this sense, the *only* Son of God. There has never been and there never will be a son quite like Jesus. And yet, the Bible teaches that God has *many* sons and daughters, and Jesus many brothers and sisters.

So *how* can this be?

Well, there are two ways a child enters a family, not just one. The most common is to be naturally born into one. An equally legitimate and increasingly popular way, however, is through *adoption*. Adoption is the process by which a child, not sharing physical genetics with a father and mother, is legally and lovingly folded into an existing family as a son or a daughter. If there are other biological children, this newly adopted sibling shares complete and equal standing: taking on the family name, receiving common provision, and benefiting from any future inheritance. I know for my wife and me, our affection for our adopted seventh child is equivalent to our other six biological children in every respect. He may look a bit different from the others on the outside (of course we all do), but he is no less a part of the family. He is a *full* Kirk.

So it is with *us*.

Adoption is the prescribed way you are spiritually born a second time—from above—into the family of God. Whether rich or poor, from high position or unemployed, whether black or white, Hispanic, or Asian...whether relatively moral or hopelessly ashamed, no one is automatically *included* or *excluded* from experiencing God the Father's adoptive grace through Jesus. Though made to know God, Adam and Eve's rebellion and our subsequent compliance orphaned us. So, it is only in response to God's Gospel call and reception of His abundant grace that any of us are folded in. As the apostle Paul explains, *"For all who are led by the Spirit of God are sons of God....you have received the Spirit of adoption as sons, by whom we cry, 'Abba! Father!' The Spirit Himself bears witness with our spirit that we are children of God"* (Romans 8:14-16). In other words, when you are adopted into God's family, you are freely given God's Spirit and the very same access to the Father's presence and affection, which the Son has always enjoyed—from all eternity. Isn't that amazing? This is precisely why Jesus invites us in Matthew 6:9 to pray as He does—*"Our Father in Heaven..."* We are given the privilege of calling God *"Abba,"* which is an intimate, endearing term like, *"Daddy!"* or *"Papa!"* And, unlike some of our earthly dads—no matter how hard they try or tried—*this* Father never plays favorites and is always available. And since He is God, God the Father can always offer you the individualized, personal attention for which you desperately long.

Always.

It is part of what makes God, God.

This surprisingly wonderful experience of adoption is beautifully illustrated in King David's (of Israel) adoption of his potential enemy, Mephibosheth. Having ascended to Saul's throne, one would have expected David to eliminate everyone from Saul's family, as they would have posed a lingering threat. And yet, out of his kindness and in keeping with his covenant promise to his best friend Jonathan (Saul's son) David pursues and finds and folds in the last remaining son of Saul's house. You can imagine Mephibosheth's fear as he was marshalled before the king. King David blows him away: *"Do not fear, for I will show you kindness for the sake of your father Jonathan, and I will restore to you all the land of Saul your* (grand) *father, and you shall eat at my table always"* (2 Samuel 9:7). Mephibosheth expects execution, yet he receives adoption. That's grace. And just to make the point, we are told twice that Mephibosheth was *"lame in both of his feet."* In other words, King David did not adopt Mephibosheth because he was particularly useful to him, he adopted him because of love—love for Jonathan and now love for Mephibosheth. Mephibosheth didn't have to earn anything, He was simply adopted by grace, as a gift. And so we are told, *"Mephibosheth ate at David's table, like one of the king's sons"* (2 Samuel 9:11). Imagine his gratitude and joy from that day on! Personal access to the king as his own father.

When was the last time you cried out to God as your very own, personal Father? When you do, His Spirit within you confirms in your heart that you belong to Him. And this belonging is not confined to today. You will always belong. In fact, as His daughter or son, you become a co-heir with Jesus Christ of everything belonging to God the Father. Hear that again, and give yourself permission to allow its truth to set deep within you:

by grace,
as an adopted child of God,
I am a co-heir with Jesus
to everything belonging to my Father.

Can you imagine the implications? Your name written in God's *Last Will & Testament*. Next to your name: *Heir.* How might really believing *that* for yourself effect how you approach God? How you approach your life? Even how you approach today? Adopted. Heir. Not because the Father is somehow cosmically obligated to fold you into His love, but because it is His great delight. As the Apostle John says: *"See what kind of love the Father has given to us, that we should be called children of God; and so we are"* (1 John 3:1). When you receive the gift of Gospel grace, *so...you...are.*

PROVISION

One of the temptations we naturally face as we begin to embrace the fatherhood of God is overestimating God's "maleness" and underestimating His "femaleness." Obviously the metaphor of "Father," not to mention "Son," is definitively male in its construct. However, we need to be careful not to attribute only traditionally male characteristics to God. God is not just a "guy," like other men we know. We call Him "He" both because that is how He has chosen to reveal Himself in the Bible, and because "it" would be an impersonal, subhuman reference. If only our language had a supra-human term for God. It doesn't.

In the opening chapter of the Bible, we learn that *"God created man in His own image, in the image of God He created him; male and female He created them. And God blessed them. And God said to them, 'Be fruitful and multiply and fill the earth'"* (Genesis 1:27-28). In other words, if God the Father had only created males, only a portion of who He is in all of His glory would have been imaged on the earth. It was only in creating male *and* female

**that the Father's glory
found its *fullest* expression.**

So, as you grow to love God as Father, it will serve you to attribute the very best of what it means to be male *and* the very best of what it means to be female. For God is simultaneously strong and wise, gentle and nurturing, pure and faithful, beautiful and mysterious. He is tougher than the hardest rock, yet more soothing than a glassy lake at sunrise, or a warm fuzzy blanket on a cold winter's night. God is *above* all things, yet *closer* to you than anyone could ever be.

He is your protector and provider, comforter and sustainer. He lovingly breaks our hardened hearts through convicting discipline and surprising mercy, and He graciously restores our broken hearts through customized care, personally tailored for us. Like us, the Father is personal, so He is able to extend love and receive love. Unlike us, however, the Father is supra-personal, so He alone is worthy of our worship! He is transcendent and imminent at the same time. Above us and right beside us.

This is such an important perspective as you turn to the Father each day in prayer. As an even greater combination of male and female than we can imagine, God the Father is uniquely equipped to fill your life with abundant, tangible goodness. In fact, He already is.

Sometimes, we just don't have
the *eyes* to see it.

Either because it is less than what other people are enjoying, which leads to discontented *jealousy*, or just less than we had hoped for, which leads to sullen *disappointment*, it is all too easy for us to overlook the abundant concrete goodness that our Father delights to fill our lives with every day. He promises the daily provision of Himself and delights to meet the common needs of our day.

"Give us this day our daily bread" (Matthew 6:11). In that famous, simple line from the prayer Jesus taught His disciples to pray, we are offered two profound insights. First, Jesus' Father is the One to whom we are to turn for all things, from the most mundane things to the most critical moments. Jesus modeled this for us over and over—rising early in the morning to greet His Father, and even seeking Him in His greatest hour of need in Gethsemane and on the Cross.

We're invited to turn to the Father
for *provision*.

Secondly, God the Father is the One from whom all blessing flows into our lives. As the Apostle James explains: *"Every good gift and every perfect gift is from above, coming down from the Father of lights with whom there is no variation or shadow due to change"* (James 1:17). In a world that is so easily thrown this way and that by the winds of uncertainty, God the Father is always dependable in His supply. He doesn't always provide everything we want, but He always provides everything we need. If we're honest, our discouragement with Him is often due to our getting these two crossed up.

Do you remember ever playing "connect-the-dots" as a child, where you would draw a line from point to point until a shape appeared? I could not more highly recommend this great *spiritual* exercise as you connect the dots of your provision every day. The more you learn to take stock of the Father's specific, palpable blessings that fill your life, the clearer *He* will appear. Try to think of tangible delights in your life right now. Let your mind cover the gamut. It could be as significant as a close, meaningful relationship—a spouse, a child, a parent, a friend—or as personal as your physical health. It could be as simple as a delicious meal or a cup of hot coffee, a cardinal flying by, or the greeting of a neighbor. While we experience the abundant resources of God every day, sadly we rarely pause long enough to take note and to give thanks. Perhaps this is why we find the Psalmist challenging his own soul to take stock of God's many blessings:

"Bless the Lord, Oh my soul,
and all that is within me, bless His holy name!
Bless the Lord, O my soul, and forget not His benefits,
who forgives all your iniquity,
who heals all your diseases,
who redeems your life from the pit,
who crowns you with steadfast love and mercy,
who satisfies you with good
so that your youth is renewed like the eagle's.
The LORD is merciful and gracious
slow to anger and abounding in steadfast love...
As a father shows compassion to his children,
so the LORD shows compassion to those who fear him."
(Psalm 103:1-5, 8, 13)

Why is it so natural for us to dwell on how God is *not* providing? Are you learning to spot how He *is*?

Beginning to *notice* **His provision**
actually catapults you
into a deeper *experience* **of God.**

And then growing heart-felt thanksgiving overflows into grateful praise! Jesus knows that we get anxious about many things. Our concern for life and loved ones is a healthy sense of responsibility. However, when we get *consumed* with concern, we malfunction and break down. We are robbed of peace and we attempt to fill our lives with things other than God and His provisions. Jesus knows this about us. So, He coaches us: *"Therefore do not be anxious, saying, 'What shall we eat?' or 'What shall we drink?' or 'What shall we wear?' For the Gentiles* (those who do not know God as Father) *seek after all these things, and your heavenly Father knows that you need them all"* (Matthew 6:31-32). Jesus knows that the way to peace is learning to enjoy and rest in God's provisions.

**Are you learning to connect the dots
of your life's *provision* to your life's *Provider*?**

Your Father in Heaven loves you more than you know. And He is gladly dropping hints all around you. Even *today*. Can you see them? Are you growing to be a mindful *Noticer*? Is "grateful" becoming your familiar posture?

PETITION

A regular joke in our home of nine is that it always seems to be time to *eat*. Surely my wife takes the brunt of this, but just when we think we've managed to prepare and serve a meal, gather the dishes and bring order to the kitchen, invariably someone says, *"I'm hungry!"* Now, in our best and most controlled moments we remind them gently that we just ate and they need to make their way out of the pantry. In our less-than-best moments we remind them with increased volume that they have already had more to eat than millions around the world, that the kitchen is closed, and that, frankly, we're not personal short-order cooks waiting on their every whim. Ok, now that's off my chest! Actually, think about it:

is that a bit of a window into the way many of us interact with God the Father?

When I look back at my prayer life, so much of it has been filled with requests, which I've convinced myself will make my life better. Because of course I know best. At least I think I do. I offer requests, one after another, as if the Father is some celestial genie I can awaken from a lamp when it suits, but gladly ignore and leave on the shelf when it doesn't. Much like your mechanic or your doctor, we can easily treat God like the Easy Button we only push when we're in a pinch. I can almost hear you saying, *"Stop meddling."* I understand. I'm almost done. If this is you, know that you are by no means abnormal. Recognizing our propensity to fill our talks with God with our "list," however, is the first step toward a healthier prayer life and a more meaningful relationship with the Father.

Thankfully, time and time again the Father *invites* our requests. To our grateful surprise, the antidote to self-focused prayer is not *withholding* what matters to us,

but simply placing it in the *context*
of what matters most to God.

A significant part of the goal of clarifying theses nine lifelong priorities of a multiplying disciple, which you are working your way through, is to increasingly have God's priorities shape your praying and therefore your living. As you grow to *love* God as Father, *honor* Jesus as King, and *follow* the Holy Spirit and as you invite His reign in your life daily, asking Him to equip you for His mission, you're certainly invited to share with Him the things that might hinder you from living it out.

And life is full of such things, isn't it? They come in the form of needs, longings, unmet desires, aches, wounds, disappointments, fears...etc. The good news is that, since you matter so much to the Father, these things matter to Him too! As the apostle Paul teaches us in Philippians, when anxiety or consuming concern rises within us—and he's assuming that it will—we're invited to tell the Father all about it in prayer: *"...in everything by prayer and supplication with thanksgiving let your requests be made known to God"* (Philippians 4:6).

We're invited.

May our hearts *never* forget that!?

Unlike weary parents who can get cranky from time to time due to the inordinate amount of seemingly incessant requests, God is always interested in and available to His children. He is eager to have His unexplainable peace *"guard your heart and your mind in Christ Jesus"* (Philippians 4:7). One of the most effective routes to His peace is *"thanksgiving."* As we grow in gratitude for who God is— unbound by circumstance—and what God is doing in our lives, He gives *perspective* to our requests.

We still have very real needs and longings. And thankfully the Christian answer isn't to stuff and bluff. That only hardens us further. Instead we are free to feel and deal, bringing our genuine self before a caring Father whose supply is plentiful and abundantly good. As Paul testifies: *"In any and every circumstance, I have learned the secret of facing plenty and hunger, abundance and need. I can do all things through Him who strengthens me"* (Philippians 4:12). And as Paul promises: *"my God will supply every need of yours according to His riches in glory in Christ Jesus"* (Philippians 4:19).

Now admittedly, as I suggested earlier, God's provision is often not *what* we had in mind, nor does it often come *when* we think best.

This is one of the hardest lessons to learn on this journey. His provision, however, does arrive, and, when we approach God as our loving Father instead of a cosmic vending machine, we find that we get more than we asked for. We get Him! You see,

God Himself is the *secret*,
to which Paul refers.

It's not some magical formula. In plenty and in want, God is our sole source of contentment. The Father personally strengthens the weary, pacifies the anxious, and satisfies the hungry. Which of these resonate with you most right now? Would you say you're weary, or anxious, or hungry? As His child, might it be time for the sun to rise again on your prayer life, to renew your conversation with the Father? I have found that God is always ready for another go. That's grace. You *can* begin again.

Perhaps a good place to start is the prayer that Jesus Himself taught the first disciples in Matthew 6:9-13. You can practice a simple three-step prayer:

DECLARE...how holy and worthy God the Father really is.

- *What do I love and cherish most about His character?*

INVITE...His will and reign to find expression in your life.

- *Where are my thoughts or actions out of alignment with His wise and good intentions for me?*

ASK...Him to *provide* today's bread, *forgive* yesterday's sins, and to *protect* you from tomorrow's temptations?

- Please provide for my most pressing needs.

- Please cleanse me of all that I've done or failed to do, and all the words I've spoken or failed to speak.

- Please guard me from the wiles of sin that would seek to lure me in and away from you.

As the Father shapes our praying, He will begin to shape our living as well. Prayer is less about convincing God to act as we would have Him, and more about humbly inviting Him to act as He sees fit. It is truly an act of faith, when you invite the Father to father you. He knows best.

DEVOTION

One of the most influential "fathers" of the early church is a man named Augustine. In his most famous book, he writes: *"You have made us for yourself, O Lord, and our hearts are restless until they find their rest in you"* (Confessions, Book I). If Augustine is accurate, and I think he is, our common discontent acts a bit like an internal homing device that sends us searching. Along the way we try many things other than the Father to quench our thirst and satisfy our soul's deepest desires. Ironically, we gladly yield our will, our mind, and our passion to things that only leave us searching for more, for deeper, instead of for that which will last.

**It is God's grace
that these things *don't* satisfy.**

For if they did, we would likely miss God, settling for fleeting surface delights over the constant and ever deepening joy of knowing and loving God as Father. Our desperate exhale finally sets in, as we grow to yield the whole of our being—our heart, our soul, and our mind—to God Himself.

Jesus was once asked in Matthew 22:36 what the *greatest*—meaning most important—commandment was. Without hesitation, He affirmed Deuteronomy 6:4-5, which He had probably grown up quoting literally every day of His life:

> *"Love the Lord your God*
> *with all your heart*
> *and with all your soul*
> *and with all your mind."*

He then adds, perhaps to our surprise: *"And a second is like it: love your neighbor as yourself. On these two commandments depend all the Law and the Prophets"* (Matthew 22:39-40). Jesus' words offer an incredibly significant clarification. One of the primary ways we love God as Father is learning to love each other as we love ourselves. In other words, the CLOSER CIRCLE (our *familial* love for those inside the faith) and the FURTHER ARROW (our *missional* love for those outside the faith) are integrally connected to the STRONGER TRIANGLE (our *childlike* love for God). We develop this connection in the chapters corresponding to those shapes. Here, however, our focus is on Jesus' call to a wholehearted devotion to God.

God's highest priority for your life
is to *love* Him.

Think about that. The most important thing in life is growing to love God as your personal Father. This is not, by the way, because of any deficit in Him, as if He *needs* love. Certainly not. According to 1 John 4:9, *"God is love,"* so it is already central to the essence of His character. We are called to love God because He's worthy and because *our* wholeness is only found in this personal exchange of divine affection. It's a gift. God graciously initiates this exchange. In the Old Testament, Israel was called to love God, but only *after* He graciously delivered them out of oppressive Egyptian captivity. In other words, love for God is not a duty you are required to summon from within you *against* your will; it is the natural answering response to receiving His love. It's all grace!

We love because He loved us *first.*

It is never the other way around. But what does it look like to cultivate a growing affection for God as Father? Well, according to Jesus, it takes everything we have. It takes us engaging the Father with all three aspects of our person—our heart, our soul, and our mind. Let's explore these three in greater depth.

When Jesus says "heart," He is referring primarily to our "will." It is the evaluative part of you that weighs options and makes decisions. Your heart is like your spiritual, central nervous system. As it goes, so goes your life. Therefore, loving God includes the yielding of your will to His. It does not require you to suppress your desires, but it also does not permit you to chart your own course. You love God by being honest with Him about what *you* want, but then surrendering your desires to what *He* wants. As Jesus modeled for us in Gethsemane: *"My Father, if it be possible, let this cup pass from me; nevertheless, not as I will, but as you will"* (Matthew 26:39). Jesus was authentic and real, yet yielded. Surrendering our autonomy (*auto* – "self," *nomos* – "law") to God's authority is not easy. Deliberately moving from having a hardened heart to having a pliable, willing heart is a process, which is essential and inevitable in the sons and daughters of God. While we *genuinely* love God at conversion, it is *incomplete*. We grow to love God more fully over a lifetime of increasing devotion.

**This development is true
of our *soul* as well.**

Since both our heart and soul are at the core of our essence as humans, we need not oversimplify where the heart ends and where the soul begins. However, if the heart primarily analyzes *external* options—choosing to pursue one path over another—perhaps the soul is a bit more *internal*, the "real you" at the depth of your being. It is where longing resides. It feels passion and emotion, remembers wounds, holds grudges, and treasures memories. Your intrinsic sense of identity, worth, and purpose emanate from your soul. It is the most deeply profound influence in your life. This is why it is no real surprise that Jesus calls us to a fully devoted expression of soul. God isn't interested in gaining a mere *religious* slice of our lives or a portion of our time. Far from it. He wants the whole of us. And loving Him looks like

**finally discovering your *real self*
in a relationship with Him.**

What keeps you from celebrating God the Father as your daily source of joy and hope, the healer of your past, and the very good designer of what lies ahead? Is your soul finding rest in God alone? Who or what has His rightful and central place in your life?

And how about your *mind*? Our whole being cannot be summarized simply by will or passion. We are thinkers and learners too. Much like the involuntary beating of our hearts, our minds are constantly *seeing* the world around us, perceiving everything. The mind acts like a sieve, straining the good from the bad, the hot from the cold, the pleasant from the alarming. We are always *considering* people, objects, environments, experiences…etc. You're doing it right now as you read this sentence. Your mind is working. It is truly one of God's most marvelous and complex gifts.

Sadly, it is never *neutral.*

In Ephesians 4:17, the Apostle Paul charges disciples of Jesus: *"…you must no longer walk as the Gentiles do, in the futility of their minds."* He calls them "darkened," "ignorant," and "callous." Instead, we are *"to be renewed in the spirit of our minds"* (Ephesians 4:23). Prior to receiving Gospel grace, our minds were clouded by the world's influence and our own self-interest and we lived accordingly. Now, however, we have been *illuminated* by God's truth and it should radically impact our choices. I don't ever find myself talking to Santa Clause because I've determined that he's a whimsical mythical character, rooted in history perhaps, but not a living being available for personal engagement. If, however, you become convinced that God has revealed Himself and can be known, then you will make it a priority to pursue Him with *all* your mind, allowing God's Truth to increasingly define "truth" for you. If you don't think the ice will hold your weight, you will not step out onto the frozen pond. If, however, you think the ice is sufficiently thick, you might romp and play a day's delight without a care in the world. Your capacity to *perceive* reality

largely shapes who you *are*
and who you are *becoming.*

As an act of love, yield your mind, all of it, to God the Father. Allow His perspective to determine yours. Allow the light of His Word to scatter the darkness. As Paul challenges us: *"Do not be conformed to this world, but be transformed by the renewal of your mind, that by testing you may discern what is the will of God, what is good and acceptable and perfect."* (Romans 12:2). As we gain God's perspective on all of life, we are equipped to better yield our greatest passions to Him, to have what matters most to Him increasingly matter most to us. In doing so, we give the Father the love He clearly deserves, and we discover that for which we've been made. Are you growing in your devotion for the Father? As you do, you'll find a growing desire to honor His Son welling up within you. To that lifelong priority we turn next.

LOVE
God as Father

HONOR
Jesus as King

FOLLOW
the Holy Spirit

"Jesus, thank You for redeeming me and defeating my enemy.

You are my risen King, reigning now in glory.

Your humility compels me to honor You
in all I think, say, and do.

Lead me into a life of growing obedience—more today than
ever."

5

HONOR

Jesus as King

Victory – Supremacy – Humility – Obedience

INTRODUCTION

"One if by land, two if by sea." This infamous line captures the simple strategy on which the hopes and dreams of a burgeoning nation rested. What began as an American protest against the British policy of taxation without colonial representation ended with the American Continental Congress' declaration of freedom and independence from British authority. In particular, the increasingly tyrannical rule of King George III. While multiple attempts were made to circumvent war, even offering an "Olive Branch" of allegiance to the King, war for independence became inevitable. As history reveals, King George severely underestimated the will and

determination of the American patriots and the British were eventually defeated.

Now, the English idea of "kingship" was not inherently misguided, but the colonists' loyalty ebbed as the injustice of its undue influence and intractable control grew. At great risk families sacrificed to cede themselves from beneath the Crown's weight. And a deep-seated suspicion of royals was woven into the molecular DNA of our national heritage.

Why is this so *important* for a disciple of Jesus?

While the original intentions of these revolutionaries were indeed justified (writes an American author!), perhaps we've tossed the proverbial "baby" out with the bathwater. In our effort to preserve self-governance through a representative democracy, we have inadvertently made the very concept of *kingship* a completely foreign and appalling one. Think about it: Does our inability to raise up righteous, faithful, generous kings mean that the structure itself is intrinsically flawed? Or, is it simply a revelation of the sinful inclination of the human heart? In other words, is the American rejection of King George's reach a rejection of kingship altogether, or do we simply long to be ruled *well*? In the end, our revolution was a righteous rejection of *bad* kingship. So, if there ever was a righteous king, a self-less, beneficent ruler whose commands only led to greater human flourishing, would that not be a king,

worthy of our allegiance?

This is precisely what the Bible claims about a first century Jewish man named Jesus. He was a man like any other. Though His heart was inclined toward God from the get go, we're assured in Hebrews 4:15 that He is able to sympathize with us because He was tempted in this life in every way that we are, yet was without sin. In other words, Jesus was certainly one of us, yet He was unlike any of us. While far beyond my capacity to comprehend, let alone explain, the Bible consistently claims that the man—Jesus of Nazareth—was completely divine. He was the second member of the Trinity—the Son of God—in person. The consistent Christian claim is that God literally stepped into time and space, the Creator arrived *in* creation *as* creation, through the historical person of Jesus. The apostle John confirms this in the opening words of his Gospel account: *"In the beginning was the Word (God's Son), and the Word was with God, and the Word was God. He was in the beginning with God. All things were made through him...And the Word became flesh and dwelt among us, and we have seen His glory, glory as of the only Son from the Father, full of grace and truth"* (John 1:1-3, 14). Jesus' divinity, His Sonship, His role in creation, and His arrival as a human being are all affirmed. The apostle Paul concurs, *"For in Him (Jesus) all the fullness of God was pleased to dwell"* (Colossians 1:19). In other words, God the Son, who has always existed in perfect concert with God the Father and God the Holy Spirit, "incarnated"—came *in the flesh*—so that we could know what God was really like. He came as a *prophet* telling us the good news of God's grace. He came as a *priest* administering God's grace to everyone who crossed His path. But He also came as a *King*.

And this is where it gets a bit *dicey*.

Jesus' claim to kingship is one of the most common objections to Christianity. As long as Jesus is just one religious guru among many, offering us insights into the good life, He's *acceptable*, or at least palatable. If, however, we're compelled to acknowledge Jesus as the One, true King ruling heaven and earth, deserving our total allegiance, *that* is to be squarely rejected. In a post-modern age dominated by religious pluralism and cultural relativism it is out of order to make exclusive claims about anything or anyone. Add to that the rugged, American individualism pulsating in our veins—land of the free, home of the brave—and it feels completely unnatural to bow to *any* king.

Yet this metaphor of royalty cannot be jettisoned so easily. The Bible doesn't present Jesus merely as a good teacher, a moral leader, or a gentle healer. Though He is all these things and more, the Bible unashamedly bestows upon Him the highest of rank, the greatest honor one could ever receive: *King*. And not just one king among many, but the *King of kings*! The apostle John refers to Jesus as *"Jesus Christ...the firstborn of the dead, and the ruler of kings on earth"* (Revelation 1:5). Or again, *"the Lamb (Jesus)...is Lord of lords and King of kings, and those with Him are called and chosen and faithful"* (Revelation 17:14). As God in person, Jesus is sovereign over all things. And He humbly yet confidently affirmed this just before ascending to the right hand of the Father: *"All authority in heaven and on earth has been given to Me"* (Matthew 28:18). Therefore, He alone is worthy, not just of our thanks, but of our *devotion*; worthy not just of our appreciation, but of our *allegiance*. Jesus *is* King and desires to be King in each of our lives.

He wants to *rule* you.

Not because it puffs up some unhealthy pride in Him, but because He knows you function best when ruled *well*. And no one rules better. He's a humble King, ruling with patience and kindness, mercy and grace. He *is* unwavering in His commitment to accomplish His mission in His world, but He graciously manages to keep our concerns a top priority along the way. He will not crush you, though He may discipline. He will gladly give you more freedom—real soul freedom—than laws ever could. But there will be proper boundaries.

As inclined as we are to self-govern, we were never made to rule ourselves. We function best when Jesus is enthroned in our lives. His *wisdom* can lead us in every decision, His *love* can anchor our soul every moment of every day, and His *power* can equip us with everything we need to carry out His mission.

He will never ask *of* you what He isn't willing to provide *for* you.

I love that. We cannot do without a king, you know? We just desperately need a *good* one. And Jesus is the very best you'll ever find. What might it look like for you to bow your knee—either for the first time or in a fresh way *today*—in honor of this King of Glory? Does it feel like a risky surrender? Might it be more risky *not* to? Let's find out together.

VICTORY

There's something about a good rivalry, found in politics and movies—sadly even in the halls of Junior High—but most obviously illustrated on the battlefields of athletics. No matter where you live or your personal interest level, you find yourself in the midst of a rivalry—history, tradition, turf, heartache, glory! Buckeyes, Big Blue. Bama, War Eagle. Cubs, Cardinals. Packers, Bears. Cowboys, Redskins. Or how about USA hockey playing against Russia? Anyone 40 and over will never forget that magical moment on ice, when a young band of nobodies took down the invincible, mighty Soviet Union (now Russia) on Olympic ice in Lake Placid, NY to advance to the Gold Medal game. Even non-hockey fans were BIG hockey fans that day. Because of rivalry.

Competition.

The thrill of marshalling everything you've got—mind, body, and heart—for a common goal, against a common opponent. Sure there's the threat of defeat, but that just keeps you motivated. And the potential for victory, bragging rights, is enough to offset the blood, sweat, and tears it often takes to get there. When you lose, it stings badly, but when you win there's something right in the world that wasn't right before you played the game. It isn't easy to explain, but *that* is sport.

And I think deep within, we're well aware that sport is just a miniature version of a cosmic contest playing out all around us, and even within us. There is a spiritual war in which we have a role to play, but in which we are first the *prize* before we are participants. Now, most of us can't imagine being the coveted trophy in any competition; that's because we tend to take our cues from the fickle estimation of our peers—up one day, down the next—rather than the consistently gracious assessment of our Maker. A kitchen table, handmade in a garage, may not be *worthy* of being sold at a local furniture store. But to the craftsman it is priceless, quickly becoming a cherished family heirloom. So it is with us, with you. A significant part of the journey you are on is discovering just how much you matter to the living God.

And really *believing* it.

Nothing communicates your personal worth more than the lengths to which God Himself was willing to go to *win* your freedom, your redemption.

If we step back for a moment to the beginning of the story in Genesis, we find our original parents, Adam and Eve, opposed by a wily enemy appearing in a Garden in the form of a serpent. God created majestic beings called "angels," giving them the critical mission of caring for a likewise glorious, but far more vulnerable, species: *humanity*. Made to reflect God's character everywhere we go, we were commissioned to multiply and fill the Earth with God's glory. But we needed assistance and angels were created to assist us. One in particular, however, chose to *oppose*. We can only guess that serving less-glorious humanity was simply too much for this angel's pride to swallow. And so, instead of carrying out the mission for which it was created, this angel—*the devil*—convinced multitudes of angels to join him in opposing God's mission in God's world. His initial tactic was to undermine our confidence in the trustworthiness of God.

God graciously provided Adam and Eve with all the trees of Eden—more than enough, designating only a single tree as off limits. This served as a daily reminder of His rightful place on the throne of their lives and their grateful dependence on His plentiful bounty. They wore a crown, but God was still King. Their derived reign in His world was a *gift* to be stewarded as they looked to Him and Him alone for wisdom and strength. Sadly, they stopped *looking*. As he had once jettisoned God's will for himself, this enemy deceived the first couple to doubt God's good intentions and to pursue their own desires instead. Ever since, each of us has wrestled with our own personal version of this initial faithless coup. What for the prince and princess must have initially felt like *freedom*—gods unto themselves—quickly felt like *bondage*. Sin rushed into the world with hurricane force, with the promised penalty of death in tow, and the war for human allegiance commenced.

Now, just to be clear, unlike most *good* rivalries, this war for the human heart is not waged between equals. Created angels, no matter how fierce, are no match for their Creator. The devil is not the complementary *yang* to God's *ying*; nor is he a suitable adversary in a cosmic dual. Even from the opening pages of the Bible, there is never a doubt as to who the victor will be. The Gospel promise of Genesis 3:15 paints a veiled, but hopeful, vision: *"I will put enmity between you* (the evil serpent) *and the woman* (Eve)*, and between your offspring and her offspring; He will bruise your head, and you shall bruise his heel."* Victory through agony. Both will be bruised or crushed, but Eve's offspring will win because He will deliver the death blow, the crushing of the head. The question is never: "Could God win?" The question is:

"How *would* **He?"**

And how would a human hero emerge as the champion through suffering? How would God's holy justice against sin and evil, *and* God's commitment to mercy co-mingle in the theatre of human history?

This is where Jesus enters the story. Rather than destroy His creation, God's chosen *game-plan* was to enter the fray Himself. His matchless holiness condemned human rebellion, but His unwavering love moved Him to shoulder His own judgment Himself. In John 3:16 we hear these familiar words: *"For God* (the Father) *so loved the world, that He gave His only Son, that whoever believes in Him should not perish but have eternal life."* And King Jesus willingly gave His life. *"No one takes it* (my life) *from me, but I lay it down of my own accord"* (John 10:18). At an incalculable cost the Father willingly sent His Son into the war, and, through an unexplainable sacrifice,

the Son died to *win* it!

"God (the Father) *saved us...not because of our works but because of His own purpose and grace, which He gave us...and which now has been manifested through the appearing of our Savior Christ Jesus, who abolished death and brought life and immortality to light through the gospel..."* (2 Timothy 1:9-10). Oh, the profound irony: human death *defeated* through Jesus' death, human sin *defeated* by Jesus acceptance of our sin and its due penalty, and humanity's villain (the devil) *defeated* by Jesus absorbing in His own flesh the full barrage of the devil's arsenal. *"Through death, Jesus destroyed the one who has the power of death, that is the devil, and delivered all...who were subject to lifelong slavery"* (Hebrews 2:14-15). As Paul affirms, *"He* (the Father) *disarmed the rulers and authorities and put them to open shame, by triumphing over them through Him* (Jesus)*"* (Colossians 2:15).

Unparalleled *victory* through
incomprehensible *agony*.

This is the profound, mysterious blessing of the Gospel. *This* is our King!

Our own sin, though alluring by its promise of liberty and satisfaction, enslaves us and leaves us desperately wanting. Only Jesus' Cross-shaped victory sets us free! Has Jesus set you free? He promises: *"If the Son sets you free, you will be free indeed"* (John 8:36). Is freedom becoming your daily song of gratitude? It can be! The fiercest war has already been waged, the greatest victory has already been secured. Rest in that. Receive and celebrate your victorious King!

SUPREMACY

In J.R.R. Tolkien's *Lord of the Rings*, defenseless Frodo Baggins makes his way to Mordor to destroy the terrible "Ring" once and for all. For his safety, Frodo is given the gift of *Gandalf the Grey*—a good wizard committed to seeing the adventure through. They naturally develop a sweet friendship along the journey, as Gandalf marvels at little Frodo's resilience and Frodo, likewise, admires Gandalf's wisdom and power. This bond makes one scene in particular gravely painful. In the face of a violent dragon, Gandalf selflessly stands in harm's way so that Frodo can escape unharmed. Just when you think he's managed to cheat death, the tail of the defeated dragon rises from the fiery pit, fatally whipping Gandalf's legs from under him, sending him down to his demise. Frodo wails in agony as his companion and guardian "angel" is now gone. It is a low moment to be sure. To the reader's delightful surprise, however, many scenes later, just when Frodo needs a miracle, Gandalf strides down a mountain on a white horse to save the day. It's Gandalf alright, but now he glows *white* instead of grey because he's gone through death and out the other side, better than ever!

The Biblical word for this is

resurrection.

It is not a return back to life as it was before; we might call that *resuscitation*. It is, instead, a full submersion into death, a puncturing of death's outer rim and a rising to new life like never before. In resuscitation the person recovers, only to face death again at a later date. In resurrection, however, death is completely drained of its power and the risen one is equipped with a new immortal body immune to the threat of ever dying again. Almost sounds too good to be true! Yet *resurrection* is precisely what the initial disciples of Jesus came to believe about their beloved Rabbi. Like Frodo, they too had experienced the disillusioning agony of their hero dying at the hands of an enemy—a Roman Cross with Jewish authorities consenting, and the devil cunningly behind it all. But also like Frodo, their misery turned into dancing as the darkness of Friday gave way to the sunrise of Sunday. Easter Sunday. Resurrection Sunday! Stone rolled away. Empty tomb. Empty grave clothes. And one, living Savior. Alive. Present to them as before, yet better than ever.

As you can imagine, Jesus' resurrection became the centerpiece of the good news the apostles proclaimed to anyone who would listen. In Acts 2, the first Christian sermon ever recorded, the apostle Peter explains that though *"lawless men"* crucified Jesus, *"God raised Him up, loosing the pangs of death, because it was not possible for Him to be held by it"* (Acts 2:24)! Believing Jesus to be the true King, Peter rightly compares Him to David, the greatest King in Israel's history. Like David, Jesus died. Yet unlike David who remains entombed in Israel, *"God raised Jesus up"* and His disciples saw Him. They are all *martyrs*—which means "witnesses." And not only of Jesus' life on the other side of death, but of Jesus' ascension. *"David did not ascend into the heavens"* but Jesus was *"exalted at the right hand of God"* (Acts 2:33-34). Or as the author of Hebrews puts it: *"After making purification for sins, He* (Jesus) *sat down at the right hand of the Majesty on High"* (Hebrews 1:3). In other words, this once crucified and risen Jesus is now enthroned in glory. Therefore, He and He alone is worthy of our constant devotion. Jesus is King above all others.

And it really matters that He *lives*.

In 1 Corinthians 15, the apostle Paul offers perhaps the briefest, clearest summary of the good news: *"Christ died for our sins...was buried...was raised on the third day...and appeared to Cephas, then to the twelve...then to more than 500 brothers at one time, most of whom are still alive"* (1 Corinthians 15:3-6). That last line is significant. When you are claiming a resurrection, without question the greatest evidence is eye-witness testimony. Paul not only claims that there were many witnesses and many appearances on different occasions, but that, even as he writes, many eye-witnesses are *"still alive."* Challenge the skeptic, Paul is saying, *"Go ask them for yourself!"* Now, some will wonder "What's the big deal? Isn't the impact of Jesus felt in modeling your life after His?" Well, *modeling* is certainly a crucial practice for disciples, but, as Paul explains, if Jesus is *not* risen, our faith is worthless because we're still in our sin. We remain bound in our original rebellion. In other words, it was one thing for Jesus to absorb in His own flesh all of our sin and all of the evil the enemy could muster, but if He remained dead, sin and death would have won;

and we would have *lost*.

The real victory of Jesus is suspended until Resurrection Sunday. His triumph over sin and death and the evil one himself could not have dodged the Cross, but neither can it be contained in the Cross alone. His Cross is the initial, necessary step in our redemption, but His resurrection completes the triumph. *"But in fact Christ has been raised from the dead, the first fruits of those who have fallen asleep. For as by a man came death, by a man has come also the resurrection of the dead. For as in Adam all die, so also in Christ shall all be made alive"* (1 Corinthians 15:20-22).

I wonder what difference it would make in your life if somehow it was proven that Jesus of Nazareth was still dead? What difference, today, do you think it should make if He's alive and reigning in glory? Admittedly we find it challenging to yield the whole of our lives to anyone other than ourselves. But reflect for a moment: If King Jesus willingly took your sin and God the Father's righteous judgment against your sin upon Himself, and if He punctured death and came out the other side alive and well, ready and eager to extend grace to you and to give you life, would He not be a King worthy of your allegiance? What might it look like today to take the humble, yielded posture of bowing your knee to His reign?

He *is* worthy.
***No one* is worthy like Jesus.**

Learning to honor Jesus as King is central to what it means to love God as Father. As Jesus Himself said: *"The Father...has given all judgment to the Son, that all may honor the Son...Whoever does not honor the Son does not honor the Father who sent Him"* (John 5:22-23). The two are inextricably linked. Nothing delights God the Father more than when we deliberately choose to honor the glorious Kingship of His Son, Jesus. In fact, this is precisely why the Father raised His Son from the dead. He wanted to enthrone Him *"at His right hand in the heavenly places, far above all rule and authority and power and dominion, and above every name that is named, not only in this age but also in the age to come.* He wanted to *put all things under His (Jesus) feet and give Him as head over all things to the church..."* (Ephesians 1:20-22). Our lives are included in the "all things" that are now to reside *under*

Jesus' supremacy. How is Jesus' kingship finding expression in your life? In what ways—and try to be specific—are you still attempting a coup, enthroning yourself? These are sobering, but ultimately, life-giving questions.

HUMILITY

Recently we did a bedroom makeover for our youngest sons. "Superheroes" is the theme. A mural of a city covers one wall while Superman and Captain America stand guard ready to defend it. I have to admit, I kinda like it! Like most kids, growing up I had a fascination with superheroes. These average looking everyday men and women who discover special capacities that make them anything but *average*. Some can fly, some are strong, some have special weapons, some are fast…etc. But the thing that really sets them apart, since even the villains are equipped with unusual talent, is their commitment to restore peace—saving the day, while ducking the acclaim. They appeal to us because they're more powerful than we can imagine, but also because they're more *humble* than we can explain. They always deploy their power for the restoration of others, not for their own self-promotion.

Could there be a more
accurate **description of King Jesus?**

In Philippians 2, Paul magnifies the inexplicable humility of Jesus. Unlike most superheroes, He didn't have just one or two "powers." He was God! All powers combined and then some. And though fully God, He willingly relinquished His high position for our sake, *"counting us more significant than Himself, looking to our interests"* instead of His own (Philippians 2:4). Ironically, Jesus' way to Glory's throne wasn't by grabbing power, but by giving it up: *"...though He was in the form of God, he did not count equality with God a thing to be grasped* (held on to)" (Philippians 2:6). Or, similarly: *"though He* (Jesus) *was rich, yet for your sake He became poor, so that you by His poverty might become rich"* (2 Corinthians 8:9). For our sake—our benefit—God the Son made Himself nothing, literally emptying Himself of eternal glory. The King of Glory willingly became a servant-leader, making *our* greatest need *His* greatest priority.

We actually catch glimpses of this on virtually every page of the four Gospels in route to the Cross. Encounter after encounter, Jesus graciously initiates contact with the marginalized and overlooked; loving those nobody loved. Jesus always took time for those whom no one had time—men, women, and children just like you and me. Always. In the opening chapters of Mark's Gospel alone, Jesus meets a man bound by an unclean spirit and graciously sets him free. He takes Peter's mother-in-law gently by the hand, healing her fever. He greets a paralyzed man lowered down to Him through a roof and surprises him by forgiving his sin and then making him walk as well. Spiritual and physical wholeness in a flash. He invites a man with a withered hand to stretch it out, and the man receives instant relief and great joy. And perhaps most compellingly, Jesus encounters a man filled with contagious leprosy. Moved with compassion, He humbles Himself and in order to make the leper clean reaches out and touches the man no one was willing to touch. King Jesus illustrated in a tangible, physical way what He came to do spiritually.

Jesus becomes *unclean*
to make us *clean.*

This is the surprising humility of the King of Glory! Jesus always ran *toward* those from whom everyone else was running away.

Now, as we consider His humility, we dare not perceive Jesus as a *soft* push over. At any moment the One who laid down His glory could have taken it up again. As Jesus would later rebuke Peter's attempt to protect him: *"Put your sword back into its place...Do you think that I cannot appeal to my Father, and He will at once send me more than twelve legions of angels"* (Matthew 26:52-53)? Imagine 50,000 angels showing up in a moment. He could have pursued a different route, but Jesus *chose* the path of humility, willingly embracing the lowest in the lowest of places, so that He might lift them up. He *is* King, but His reign is unexpectedly gentle and humble. In fact, He demonstrated this publically as He strode into Jerusalem on a hapless donkey just days before His Cross.

Israel had longed for their Messiah—the Christ, the anointed King—for generations. Many were finally convinced that Jesus was the "one." However, they imagined a strong, conquering King— riding more of a steed than an ass—who would smash their enemies to pieces and lift them up above the nations. They were partially right. He *was* the promised Messiah. He *was* strong. He would conquer and lift up the bowed down. But His reign would not be inaugurated through a violent act of aggression, but through a dramatic display of *affection*—His own sacrifice. The only one in human history unfamiliar with sin deliberately chose to become fully acquainted with *all* of our sin, so that He might lift us up. You might read that sentence a second time. Imagine the entirety of human sin gathered into one place, piled upon one set of shoulders?

Now, that's not *soft*!

That takes strength and power and humility the likes of which the world has never known. It is no wonder that God the Father was so delightfully pleased in His Son that as Paul says: *"He highly exalted Him and bestowed on Him the name that is above every name, so that at the name of Jesus every knee should bow...and every tongue confess that Jesus Christ is Lord, to the glory of God the Father"* (Philippians 2:9-11). In view of His unmatched humility, God re-glorified the Son—joyfully restoring to Him the glory He knew before time began. So what *difference* does this make for you and me?

Well, bowing by force of arms is something we will all try to avoid. But what about bowing to a King who was willing to bow Himself? Not just bowing the "religious" part of you—giving King Jesus a nod here and there when it conveniently suits, but intentionally learning to bring each part of your life before Jesus every day. It all matters to Him. You, matter to Him. You might try incorporating a simple prayer like this one:

> *Here's my calendar, Jesus, I want to honor You with my time.*
> *Here's my wallet, I want to honor You with my resources.*
> *Here's my past, I want to heal and honor You with my future.*
> *Here's my sin, I confess it and want to honor You by turning from it.*
> *Here's my thought-life. Here are my dreams.*
> *Here's what I feel You want me to do, that I am unwilling to do.*
> *And here's what I feel You want me to avoid that I still pursue.*
> *Here's me. All of me.*
> *I wouldn't risk bowing to anyone else.*
> *No other king is worthy.*
> *You, humble, mighty King Jesus, are the only one.*
> *Your name, Jesus, is the only name in heaven and on earth worthy of my allegiance.*
> *Take your rightful place on the throne of my life.*

Imagine how differently your life might look were that your daily posture? It *can* be. It's a process. Thankfully, our King is patient.

OBEDIENCE

True confession: even though I grew up in a Christian family, somehow I never understood that "Christ" was *not* Jesus' last name. I thought He was *Mr. Christ*, like my neighbor was *Mr. Bruckmann*. I've since discovered that "Christ" is a title, not a name, referring to Jesus' position, not His family line. He is God's anointed King. That's why I have found it helpful to refer to Him as *King Jesus*—sovereign over all things and the personal Lord of my life. The longer I follow Jesus as a disciple, however, the more I realize that what you *call* Him is far less important than how you *respond* to Him. It's easy to sing songs that declare His reign in our lives and affirm sermons that celebrate His risen, kingly status. The far more important question, however, is:

**Is *who* He is
shaping *how* I live?**

In the end, Jesus is less impressed with our capacity to *name* Him, and more delighted in our willingness to *obey* Him.

Let's face it. Obedience is challenging for most of us. For some it's more nature; for others it's more nurture. But for most it's a combination of the two. Our self-inclined heart does not *naturally* want to do what others want. Unless, of course, there's something in it for us. But then that's a form of *manipulation*, not obedience. Some of us grew up under controlling parents, unwavering in their demands, which just made disobedience that much more appealing. So often our circumstantial rebellion is less about a particular "act," and more about an iron-will, determined to go our way in defiance of having someone *over* us. We simply don't yield easily. I don't. Anyone who knows me would gladly testify. I think we *all* wrestle with this. I have never met anyone who doesn't struggle with self-inclination and some form of rebellion. Adam and Eve wrote this into our story in the beginning and we've all contributed our personal chapters. In some ways, we're still writing them.

But this is where King Jesus wants to write a *new* story.

Though equal to His Father in every way, Jesus was willing to yield to the Father's will because He knew that His Father's way led to life, and life abundant. It was His joy to obey His Father, even when it came to the excruciating choice in the Garden of Gethsemane the night before the Cross. Now "joy" might be an overstatement, but as Jesus Himself said, *"Not my will, but your will be done!"* In that one line Jesus was communicating an honest and a surrendered will. This may seem blasphemous to you, but I don't think Jesus *wanted* to die. I think He wanted to live like the rest of us. Unlike the rest of us, however, He wanted to *obey* more than He wanted anything else. Obedience is life and Jesus knew that full well.

Is there anyone more qualified to call for our growing obedience as sons and daughters of a loving Father then the obedient Son of God who blazed the trail Himself? Unlike the first Adam, this *new* Adam made obeying God His top priority. Before we give our lives to Jesus, we trust our own wisdom and reserve obeying God for fools. When you become His disciple, however, everything is turned upside down.

Or should we say, right side *up*?

As you listen to Him and follow Him, Jesus teaches and trains you to see obedience as true wisdom and rebellion as life-taking folly. In fact, in Matthew 7:21, at the end of His longest recorded sermon, Jesus offers this sobering promise: *"Not everyone who says to me, 'Lord, Lord' will enter the Kingdom of Heaven, but the one who does the will of my Father who is in heaven."* Our lip service isn't genuine unless it is followed by growing obedience. He even offers a compelling word picture, comparing a wise man who builds a house on a rock foundation with a foolish man who builds on sand. When the storms of life arrive unannounced, and they always do, the *Rock*-House prevails while the *Sand*-House is leveled. What is the difference between the two houses?

In which do you *live*?

Jesus explains that both builders *hear* His words, but the fool and his house washes away because he doesn't *do* them. The wise man survives and his house stands firm because He *does*. As Jesus boldly declares: *"If you keep my commandments, you will abide in my love, just as I have kept my Father's commandments and abide in His love"* (John 15:10).

Sobering stuff. Now, there are two potential dangers we want to avoid as we respond to Jesus' teaching. First, some of us will be inclined to think that receiving Gospel grace gets us *in*, but obedience produced by our own sheer will power is what *keeps* us in.

Good luck with *that* theology.

Actually, that perspective is far more popular than you might think. Religious people try it every day. Sadly, however, this approach leads to swift exhaustion and terrible disappointment as your manipulative concessions rarely lead to the "full joy" Jesus intends to give you. Instead, you feel as if God has let you down. Yet, as we said before, God is not a celestial genie. Which means your obedience is not the equivalent of rubbing the lamp and getting God to respond to your every whim. That's not how this works.

But a second response is equally dangerous. Since the kind of obedience Jesus calls for seems *impossible,* some conclude that it is not worth our serious effort. Whereas the first response leads to self-righteousness and eventual frustration, this second response leads to spiritual apathy and indifference. Common among many who name the name of Jesus, is a complacency that says,

"Since I can't obey it *all*,
I won't obey *at* all."

Obedience becomes optional for the radical or the really committed disciple. Be assured, King Jesus does not see it that way.

Being a Christian means you *are* a disciple of Jesus. There's no distinction between obedient ones and disobedient ones. Growing obedience is necessary and expected of any and all disciples. As Jesus says: *"Whoever has my commandments and keeps them, he it is who loves me...if anyone loves me, he will keep my word"* (John 14:21, 23). But, and this will lead us to consider our sixth lifelong priority — *following the Holy Spirit* — King Jesus never intends to have you obey on your own. He is as committed to equipping you for obedience along the journey as He was committed to saving you at its inception.

**And there's *always* grace
for falling short.**

Every day is filled with new expressions of God's grace. Every sin in your past and all of those just up ahead have been fully dealt with through the King's Cross.

Take stock for a moment: When it comes to learning to obey King Jesus, would you say your heart leans *closed* or *open*? Perhaps you can at least confess that, while you want to honor His reign in every aspect of your life, you need His assistance in knowing what that should look like. I am confident that He will eagerly respond to such a yielded spirit. And He will gladly equip you by His Holy Spirit to grow you and mature you into an obedient, faithful disciple. This indispensable life of the Spirit is that which we turn to next.

FOLLOW
the Holy Spirit

"Holy Spirit, thank you for your constant presence within me.

Guide me today in the way I should go, as I follow your lead.

Make me wise and responsive to your promptings.

Strengthen me and bear the fruit of Jesus' character in me today."

6

F O L L O W

the Holy Spirit

Indwelling – Guidance – Wisdom – Power

INTRODUCTION

Though I couldn't have diagnosed myself at the time, apparently as a child I struggled with a significant dose of "separation anxiety." This primarily manifested itself with my mother. As long as she was at home or as long as I was *with* her, I was OK. But the moment she left—even to just go to the bank for a little while—I was a mess. I can honestly remember rounding second base in my back yard during a Wiffleball game, seeing her pull out of the driveway, and then making a straight bee-line past the pitcher, through home plate and up the blacktop with tears rolling down my eyes for fear that I might never see her again. I understand now that that was the height of delusion, but it was *my* reality. I've never quite identified the source of my disorder, but I had a strong *need* to be with my mom in particular. Thankfully, I have either outgrown it or been healed from it.

I have often wondered, however, in my adult years if some of that desire for "presence" is not actually built-in to the wiring of what it means to be *human*. Most extroverts are quick to agree. And while you might be an introvert with your emotional and relational batteries often recharging *apart* from people, my guess is you would not do well to be left alone for too long. This was starkly illustrated by Chuck Noland, Tom Hanks' stranded character in *Castaway*, who treated a volleyball like a person he named "Wilson" in order to remain semi-sane.

Presence is *that* important.

We are designed to function best with *another*, in relationship. Since Father, Son, and Holy Spirit have always known each other's presence, and since we are made in God's image, there are probably theological origins for this innate desire in us.

I imagine Jesus' first disciples endured a fair amount of separation anxiety as the shadow of the Jerusalem Cross fell across their Rabbi's future. As a nation, they had longed for His arrival for centuries, so I would imagine they felt truly privileged to be a part of the generation that saw His literal face. He was no longer a wished-for promise; He was reality in the flesh. They knew Him personally: how tall He was, what His hair looked like, how He liked to dress. They knew His food and wine preferences, when He liked to rise and turn in for the night. They knew Him. If they heard Him laugh from the other room, they'd have known it was Him. In fact, the Gospels suggest that Jesus was with them on a daily basis and they followed Him everywhere He went. Even at one point, when Jesus was briefly transfigured in glory with Moses and Elijah appearing on a mountain top, the few disciples present wanted to set up tents and campout indefinitely. As long as they were *with* Jesus, they were alright. So, the thought of that ever coming to an end must have filled them with a very great sadness. That is, until Jesus began speaking of a great *mystery* they'd soon experience.

In John 14 Jesus says to His disciples, *"I will ask the Father, and He will give you another Helper, to be with you forever"* (John 14:16). A few verses later He identifies this "Helper" as the Holy Spirit. And the insight is that Jesus is the first of *two* Helpers, rather the only one. In other words, God the Father's plan was to send the Son to *accomplish* our redemption—the Cross and Resurrection—but then to quickly follow up with the Spirit, who would personally *apply* King Jesus' redemption to our lives. And notice, Jesus, knowing of their need for presence *and* permanence, promises that the Spirit's company will last *forever*. Jesus wasn't overlooking their emotions; He was lovingly preparing them for life without Him. Or should we say,

life *with* Him
even after He's gone.

Jesus acknowledges their ache: *"Sorrow has filled your heart. Nevertheless…it is to your advantage that I go away, for if I do not go away, the Helper will not come to you. But if I go, I will send Him to you"* (John 16:7). Now, *advantage* seems like a bit of an overstatement, especially for those first disciples who had Jesus all to themselves. How could Jesus' absence possibly benefit them? Only if the Spirit's promised presence were to give them, and future disciples like them, even *greater* access to Jesus than they'd ever known. *This* is precisely the point. Jesus had taught them many things, modeled for them what it looks like to love God wholeheartedly and to love people selflessly. However, now it was time for Him to take this modeling to a whole new level. As John explains, *"...having loved His (Jesus) own who were in the world, He loved them to the end"* (John 13:1). All the way. Through His Cross, Jesus demonstrated abandon and sacrifice the likes of which the world had never seen. And it was His intention to then rise to His glorious throne and continue to live out His mission in His world—*through* His disciples, *by* the power of the Holy Spirit.

Jesus would shift from serving as their Rabbi to serving as their King, and ours. By His Spirit *within* us He would not only lead us to obey, but enable our obedience. By His Spirit, King Jesus is able to be fully present and available with undivided attention to each and every disciple that bows the knee to His glorious and gentle reign. That was true in the first century and that remains true today for you and me.

That is the *advantage* of which Jesus spoke.

In fact, the final words of the risen King Jesus on the earth before ascending to the right hand of God the Father are: *"And behold, I am with you always, to the end of the age"* (Matthew 28:20). As they carried out His mission of making disciples—leading new ones *into* faith, and training existing ones *in* the faith—they would still know His presence, even after His departure. And His presence would not only be *with* them, it would be *in* them. And in *us*! Are you open to having God Himself reside within you? Without Him, the Christian journey feels a lot like dry religion. With Him, however, it's an exciting adventure. To this adventure, we turn next.

INDWELLING

There are only 124 astronauts who have orbited earth more than once and I had the privilege of getting to know one of them quite well. At one point I asked this United States Air Force Colonel about His experience of God while looking back at planet earth from his shuttle. His answer surprised me. *"Oh, it was amazing! But it wasn't more amazing than it is every day on earth. Because God is with me here just the same as He was with me there!"* I was stopped in my tracks. What an insight. The thrill of a particular moment — whether watching a gorgeous sunset over the Pacific, smelling the sweet pine in the mountains of Colorado, or floating 99 miles above earth encircling the planet in about 22 minutes — whatever the thrill, our experience of God as disciples of Jesus can remain constant because God Himself resides *within* us everywhere we go. *Every* moment — from the most profound to the most mundane — serves as another opportunity to engage God and cultivate this most important relationship.

Remember, Jesus said it was better that He go away — to His throne in Glory — so that He might send His Spirit to be with us...and even *in* us. *"You know Him (the Spirit of Truth), for He dwells with you and will be in you"* (John 14:17). If Jesus had somehow chosen to remain on earth, we would only be able to know His personal presence by traveling to be where He is. However, instead, through His indwelling Spirit, Jesus is always present wherever *we* are. And not just *with* us, but *in* us. And for the first disciples this had to be an almost impossible teaching to absorb.

From beginning to end, the story of the Bible catalogues the presence of God with His people. In the opening chapter of Genesis, we find Him present with Adam and Eve in the Garden of Eden. And then at the end of redemptive history, we hear this hope-filled glorious promise: *"Behold, the dwelling place of God is with man. He will dwell with them, and they will be His people, and God Himself with be with them as their God"* (Revelation 21:3). In other words, the centerpiece of God's story is God's presence with His people. That's where *wholeness* — in Hebrew "shalom," in Greek "peace" — resides. God's presence. In the beginning, everything was just right, and in the end it will be just right again.

But what about in the *meantime*?

That is the important question for us today. What about right *now*? Are we left only to pine for the good ole days of Eden or long for the promised days of New Creation? Well, that pining and longing is certainly justified, but God has graciously provided a way into His presence in the interim.

Let's step back again to gain some perspective. Initially, God chose Israel to be the people of His presence, through whom He would bring blessing to the nations. He never chose Israel because its people were more qualified than those of other nations, nor did He intend for Israel to keep His blessings to themselves. On the contrary, Israel was to serve as a channel of His presence and love to the watching world. Since it was as unholy as any other nation, however, God always needed to *cloak* His presence. Not because He wanted to hide from His people, but because He wanted to *preserve* them. In the revealed presence of His Glory — His pure, uncontaminated holiness — human sin cannot stand.

So God mercifully *veiled* His glory until sin was dealt with once and for all.

Along the way, He met with Moses—Israel's deliverer—but *cloaked* Himself in a burning bush and a cloud at the top of Mt. Sinai. He was present among Israel in their Exodus to the land of promise, but *cloaked* Himself in a moveable tent—a Tabernacle. He led them personally, but *hid* in a pillar of fire and a cloud of smoke along the way. Again, not because God didn't want them to know Him, but precisely because He did! It just wasn't time yet for human sin to be removed, so it wasn't time for *immediate* access. Of course that time would come through the Cross of Jesus.

But not *yet*.

Once in Jerusalem, a permanent Temple with three concentric sections replaced the portable Tabernacle, the holiest section—the *Holy of Holies*—being reserved for God alone. Imagine a sixty-foot high, thirty-foot wide, three-inch think curtain serving as a necessary partition between God's holy presence and unholy Israel.

That is, until one *historic* Friday.

In Matthew 27 we read of Jesus' sacrifice for human sin and its dramatic effect: *"Jesus...yielded up His spirit* (in death). *And behold, the curtain of the temple was torn in two, from top to bottom"* (Matthew 27:50-51). What a remarkable sign that the barrier of human sin had been overcome. The presence of God was finally available to those Jewish and non-Jewish disciples—then and now—who gladly receive the cleansing grace of King Jesus' Cross.

It is against this Old Testament backdrop that you and I can appreciate the promised gift of the Holy Spirit placed *within* us. Though the first disciples struggled to wrap their mind around it, in time they understood. The apostle Paul reminds Christians: *"Do you not know that you are God's Temple and that God's Spirit dwells in you? God's Temple is holy, and you are that temple"* (1 Corinthians 3:16-17). Or similarly, *"Do you not know that your body is a temple of the Holy Spirit within you, whom you have from God? ...so glorify God with your body"* (1 Corinthians 6:19-20). In other words, since you've been so thoroughly cleansed of your sin—made *holy* by the blood of the Lamb—you no longer need to be preserved *from* God's presence. Now He accompanies you everywhere you go, delighting to make His home *in* you.

As precious as the physical Temple was to Judaism for so many centuries, the teaching of Jesus and the apostles is that, in Jesus, the entire point of the Temple was fulfilled and, through the personal, abiding presence of the Holy Spirit, its necessity is eclipsed. The stone and mortar was a foretaste,

Jesus and the Holy Spirit are the *real* thing!

No wonder an astronaut can enjoy God as much in his front yard as in outer space. Have you ever considered that you are the personal residence of the holiness of God? Do you believe that? How might that reality impact your relating to Him and your thoughts and activities each day?

GUIDANCE

Perhaps my greatest pet-peeve is getting lost. Whether it is the wasted time or the feeling of being out of control, few things get under my skin more quickly than vainly roaming around in the wrong direction. Even as I write this I am looking at Fox Mountain in Colorado where I was perilously lost during a *quick* hike. This is why the invention of the iPhone, and Siri in particular, has been such a blessing. When it is time to travel somewhere unfamiliar, you just plug in the coordinates and off you go. Along the way you're given updates as to your progress and how far you are from your next turn. If by chance you take a "wrong" turn off the prescribed course, Siri quickly adjusts, reroutes, and gets you back on track. Good as new. Siri is also the first to welcome you to your destination and you almost feel a sense of accomplishment as Siri affirms your success. Alright, I know it's a thing, not a person. But it is a helpful tool because we are prone both

to being *ignorant* of the right path
and veering *off* the right path

once we know the way. This is true with our geographical sense of direction, and it is equally true in our spiritual journey as disciples of King Jesus.

At great risk of oversimplification, the Holy Spirit within you is intended to serve as a spiritual version of Siri. Perhaps the Bible's most prolific metaphor for getting to know God and becoming who He made you to be is that of a *journey*. This is the clear inspirational source of Tolkien's *Lord of the Ring's* Trilogy, which chronicles the daunting quest a few Hobbits reluctantly, but willingly undertake. Leaving the comfort of home, they make their way to frightening Mordor where they destroy the source of evil plaguing their land. They return to the Shire having secured a better life. While their journey requires a whole fellowship of individuals to complete, it largely rests on the wise direction of on old wizard, named Gandalf.

Similarly, a *journey* is the central word-picture
of the Old Testament.

God's presence leads Israel out of bondage and into freedom through the Exodus. Their path had stages: *captivity, deliverance, freedom, wilderness,* and then finally *inheritance* in the Promised Land. And, as the writers of the New Testament attempt to explain a disciple's life, a similar course is charted.

Our *captivity* comes through Adam's sin. We are born into it and confirm it by our own sinful choices. Our *deliverance* comes graciously through the Cross and Resurrection of Jesus, which unshackle the chains of our guilt and shame, launching us into new found freedom. As Jesus Himself says, *"So if the Son sets you free, you will be free indeed"* (John 8:36). Or likewise Paul, *"For freedom Christ has set us free"* (Galatians 5:1). Forgiveness of sin and a restored relationship with the One who made you. *This* is the gift of freedom. But Paul quickly warns us of something very important, *"For you were called to freedom, brothers. Only do not use your freedom as an opportunity for the flesh* (self-inclination opposed to God), *but through love serve one another"* (Galatians 5:13). In other words,

learn from Israel's mistake in the wilderness.

They did not remain faithful to God, and so they wandered around aimlessly for many years, filling their lives with things that did not satisfy. As a disciple of Jesus on your way to your eternal inheritance—*Heaven* at death and eventual *New Creation* when King Jesus returns to restore all things—don't get lost in self-inclined pursuits. Instead, embrace your new freedom as an opportunity to finally become who God made you to be: in particular, a lover of those around you. *That* is what the "now" time is supposed to be about. As Gandalf says to Frodo, *"All we have to decide is what to do with the time that is given to us."* This leg of the journey is about loving God and loving people. Thankfully, we're not left to find our own path.

**The Holy Spirit is present *within* you to
lead you on your way.**

One of the *advantages* of King Jesus returning to Glory and sending His Spirit into the hearts of His disciples, is that He can offer us personal guidance in all things, at all times. This is why Jesus promises, *"the Helper, the Holy Spirit...will teach you all things and bring to your remembrance all that I have said to you"* (John 14:26). Or in John 16: *"When the Spirit of Truth comes, He will guide you into all truth...whatever He hears He will speak...He will glorify me, for He will take what is mine and declare it to you"* (John 16:13-14). In other words, Jesus' mentoring did not come to an end in His departure; it just entered a new phase, less external and more internal, where the Spirit communicates God's will to the deepest parts of us:

This is what's true.
This is what's beautiful.
This is what's right.
This is what's important.
This is what love looks like in this moment.
This is what love needs to look like with that person over there.

Like Siri, the Holy Spirit plays the role of *compass* in the human heart. Even in the 21st Century, Jesus is alive and well and through His Spirit—and the Scripture He inspired—Jesus gladly disciples those who follow Him. Learning to follow the Holy Spirit, moment by moment, is what following King Jesus looks like until He returns.

It is fitting that the apostle Paul employs *journey* language in Romans 8 and in Galatians 5. In Romans 8 he writes: *"For those who live according to the flesh set their minds on the things of the flesh, but those who live according to the Spirit set their minds on the things of the Spirit"* (Romans 8:5). Who are you allowing to set the course of your life; your days and weeks in your calendar, which *become* your life? Are you led primarily by what *you* want, or what you think you need? Or, are you increasingly discovering what God wants and following His Spirit into that?

Viewed through a slightly different metaphor, how is your gait?

We each have a natural rhythm
to how we walk.

People in college used to say they knew it was me across campus because of my pace and my step. How do you step? Do you walk through your day set on what you intend to accomplish, or are you beginning to yield your gait to the rhythm of the Spirit? In Galatians 5, Paul puts it this way: *"But I say, walk by the Spirit, and you will not gratify the desires of the flesh"* (Galatians 5:16). Of course, the inverse is also true. If you neglect the leading of the Spirit in your life, your default will be to pursue your own satisfaction— using things, experiences, and, sadly, even people to your own ends. Yet, as you learn to live in sync with the heartbeat of the Spirit, you can actually be used by God in other people's lives to *His* end. *This* is the freedom for which we have been delivered. *"If we live by the Spirit, let us also walk by the Spirit"* (Galatians 5:25). It is God's abundant grace that we can! Are you learning to discern the guidance of the Holy Spirit? You might ask a disciple of Jesus you respect what that looks like in their lives.

WISDOM

I remember a moment years ago with one of my young daughters. I think she was 3. We were talking about God and at one point I asked her, *"You know where you come from, right?"* I wanted her to realize that the One who made the moon and the stars was the same One who put her together. That it was His delight to create her, just as she was. But you know kids; they say the wildest things. She looked up at me and as seriously as she could answer she said, *"From Walmart?"* My wife and I just howled. It was one of the cutest conversations ever. I followed up by asking her if she thought we bought her, and she said we just picked her right off the shelf. Oh, I love these honest exchanges with little kids. They have a growing, but still very limited, understanding of the way the world works.

The way *life* works.

They are *sophomores* in the truest sense of the term. "Soph" means *wisdom*. "Mores" comes from "moron," which of course means *fool*. Wise...fool. They're not babies anymore—they can get around and reason and talk—but they're not quite old enough to make much *sense* of anything. Which makes for hilarious conversations. We've had the treasure of seven comical journeys through this stage of life, and I look forward to doing it all over again with grandkids, if the Lord wills.

Think about it: Isn't it fitting that the Tenth Grade bears the name *sophomore*? No longer a nervous, naïve freshman, but not really serious like a junior, or confident like a senior. Wise-fools are given twelve months to strut their stuff. They think they've got it *all* figured out, but sobering reality is right around the corner. They soon discover they're still learning how life *really* works.

Sophomore **is a pretty good depiction of
a new disciple of Jesus as well.**

When we come to faith, we naturally have a very limited understanding of who God is, what He wants for us, and what His mission in His world is all about. And that's alright. There is nothing wrong with being spiritually naïve out of the gate. We are "newborns" after all, and we have to go through the stages of development just like we did in childhood. The exciting thing is we *can*! You *can* develop spiritually, you *can* grow and mature, because God's very own Spirit dwells within you, giving you daily insight into the mind and heart of God.

This is one of the greatest gifts the Holy Spirit is eager to give you. Insight, a live "look-in" to what God is really like, and what God might really *want* in a given moment. Whether that's at the sink doing dishes, lining up a ten-foot putt at the local course, driving to work in heavy traffic, or lying in bed wide awake at three a.m. retooling the family budget. The Holy Spirit has this uncanny capacity to make you wise—helping you identify what matters most to God, charting a course and taking the next step. As the apostle Paul prays, *"...that you may you be filled with the knowledge of His will in all spiritual wisdom and understanding, so as to walk in a manner worthy of the Lord, fully pleasing to Him, bearing fruit in every good work and increasing in the knowledge of God"* (Colossians 1:9-10). Isn't this the journey we are all on as disciples of Jesus?

None of us have cornered the market on knowing God. We are works in process. That's what the original word "disciple" means— a *learner*.

Far from being experts, we are *learning* **Jesus.**

It's a daily journey of getting to know God better: gaining His perspective on your life, discovering what He wants, sensing His promptings, and following through. We don't do this perfectly, but are you intentionally making decisions with *His* will in mind? Are you eager to live *today* in a way that brings Him glory—that demonstrates how great God is, how wise and kind and generous and trustworthy? These are challenging questions for all of us. Paul's words here, however, give us hope. You actually *can* live a life that brings God pleasure. You *can* live a fruitful life today, filled with good, meaningful work.

And the Holy Spirit is the *key*.

He is your personal, constant link to the mind and heart of God.

This is precisely what Paul teaches in 1 Corinthians 2. Paul's great challenge in mentoring these young "learners" of Jesus is that, being so heavily influenced by Greco-Roman philosophy, they thought they had already *arrived*. They thought they were wise—understanding the gods and how life worked best. But they were really *sophomores* (wise-guys). Through reason and stoicism—logic and emotional indifference—the Corinthian populace thought they'd discovered the virtuous life. In the process, however, they made it virtually impossible to embrace a crucified and risen King. Especially one who found more life in giving Himself away than in taking whatever He could.

**The unreasonableness of the Cross and
the self-emptying love of King Jesus
was simply too *foolish* to believe.**

And yet, as Paul explains: *"The natural person does not accept the things of the Spirit of God, for they are folly to him, and he is not able to understand them because they are spiritually discerned"* (1 Corinthians 2:14). In other words, you can be a genius and not know God. And you can be amateurish and know Him very well. It all comes down to your reception of, and responsiveness to, the promptings of God, the Holy Spirit.

According to Paul, the Holy Spirit within you tunes the frequency of your heart and mind to the frequency of God's: *"No one comprehends the thoughts of God except the Spirit of God. Now, we have received...the Spirit who is from God, that we might understand the things freely given us by God"* (1 Corinthians 2:11-12). Ironically, Paul employs logic to convince the logical of the spiritual. His point is that your personal access to God, through His Spirit, ought to embolden your confidence that God is knowable and that God's *ways* are knowable. If we were left to simply guess what God desired for us each day, it would be a frustrating roll of the dice or flip of the coin. Hitting and missing.

Mostly *missing.*

But instead, since you have God's Word—the Bible—inspired by the same Holy Spirit dwelling within you, and since you have immediate access to the will of the living God through His Spirit, you can grow and mature as a wise son or daughter, brother or sister.

I know that we don't live *with* Jesus like the first century learners. But in a sense, we can live with Him just as intimately.

And perhaps *more* **so.**

The Holy Spirit gives us access to the deepest parts of Him. After all, *"We have the mind of Christ,"* Paul says (1 Corinthians 2:16). When was the last time you invited the Holy Spirit to reveal God to you? His character, His will, His joy, His glory? Tune in and *respond.* He's busy all around you and eager for you to join Him. Are you learning to follow the Holy Spirit? Oh, and by the way, my little daughter from Walmart? Her name is *Sophie*—wisdom!

POWER

I had the unfortunate experience of destroying my iPhone by submerging it in water. It happened jumping into a pool fully clothed to save my sinking three-year-old, so it was worth it. When I hopped out, however, and checked to see if it was working, a few dashes appeared briefly on the screen and then...*nothing*. It was gone. We did the whole "dry rice" fix, but even three days later, *nothing*. No life. Not even a smidgen of a *sign* of life. It was lost. The phone was dead and no longer of any use. Cell-phones have been an amazing technological invention but they're not self-generating. They still require *juice* to function properly.

As disciples of Jesus, so do *we*.

Paul writes: *"My little children, for whom I am again in the anguish of childbirth until Christ is formed in you"* (Galatians 4:19). Transformation. *That* is the goal of our discipleship—that the character of Jesus Himself would be formed *in* us, and manifested *through* us. But how do we get there? Well, like anything else you have a role to play, but the primary source of change in your life is the Holy Spirit. As Paul says, *"we all...are being transformed into the same image* (of Jesus) *from one degree of glory to another. For this comes from the Lord who is the Spirit"* (2 Corinthians 3:18). In other words, your transformation is God's work in you, not your work for God. The Holy Spirit is committed to giving you new capacity. As Paul contends, *"...for it is God who works in you, both to will and to work for His good pleasure"* (Philippians 2:13). New desire, new ability — wanting to please God and actually pleasing Him — is the work of *His* Spirit in *your* life. It's why Paul prays for the Christian disciples in Ephesus, *"...may God grant you to be strengthened with power through His Spirit in your inner being"* (Ephesians 3:16). It's also why he is so confident that God is *"able to do far more abundantly than all that we ask or think, according to the power at work within us"* (Ephesians 3:20). Power, is the Greek word *dunamis*, which we know as "dynamite." Not just a little extra kick every once and a while, but the same explosive power that called Creation into being and raised King Jesus from the dead. That power resides within you by the Spirit. Which certainly begs the question:

Why so *little* change?

Sometimes we see dramatic shifts in a disciple's life, but often we see very little movement. What attests for the difference? Well, that is indeed a great mystery, and I'm not certain I know the answer. However, the, longer I follow Jesus, the more convinced I am it has to do with our engagement of the Spirit. The cultivation of a regular rhythm of:

faith,

prayer,

expectancy,

and *follow through.*

First, do you *believe* that God the Holy Spirit is alive within you and can literally transform you from one degree of glory to another? Is that just theological jargon or do you believe that could be true for you? Secondly, are you *praying* that He will transform you? Are you learning to ask God daily to form the character of Jesus in you, animating you from within? Third, are you *expecting* that He will? One of the reasons we see so little spiritual development in our lives is that we've stopped anticipating it. Initially, when you come to faith, there's fresh energy and enthusiasm to grow. But for so many in time that wanes and we plateau, settling for incremental growth that's often of little consequence. We start going through the religious motions and we call it "discipleship." We may be stirred deep within by a sermon, or a book, or a worship song, but the "high" passes quickly as we don't expect to be changed.

**Which leaves us with the final,
crucial step**—*follow through.*

It's one thing to believe and to even pray and begin to expect, but are you learning to take risks: stepping out of your comfort-zone to follow the Spirit into the radical, joy-filled life King Jesus died to give you? Just like physical fitness cannot just *happen* without diet and exercise (Oh, how we wish it could!), so, too, spiritual growth cannot occur without follow-through. When the Spirit prompts you—as you believed He *could*, and as you prayed and expected He *would*—how do you respond? Is it, *"Maybe later? Maybe not that much? Maybe someone else?"* Or is it increasingly,

Yes, Lord. I'm in.
I'll give that a try.

I'll give this away.
I'll forgive this wrong.
I'll make that call.
I'll take the time, show some interest.
I'll trust you.
I'll bring my sin to light.

And on and on the list goes. For the Spirit has a great deal of work to accomplish in all of us. Believe me you are not alone. If we don't believe, or pray, or expect, or follow through, growth is nearly impossible. If on the other hand, and I am banking my life on this, if you begin to learn to take God at His Word (which means it's already on your heart), if you pray faithfully that His will would be done, if you expect Him to do great things, and if you respond swiftly to the promptings of His Spirit, your growth will be dramatic and God will receive the glory that is His due. Don't you want that?

Aren't you tired of just *checking* the box,
and *going* through the motions?

Don't you want to believe that there's more? There is! And remember, it's not more for you to produce for God, but more He intends to produce *through* you. Both Jesus and Paul explain this great mystery through the everyday, agricultural image of a vineyard—vines, branches, and fruit. Discovering which one you are makes all the difference.

Jesus says: *"I am the vine; you are the branches. Whoever abides in me and I in him, he it is that bears much fruit, for apart from me you can do nothing"* (John 15:5). Allow Jesus to disciple you through this one sentence. He teaches us three important lessons. First, He is the source of life; we are not. Like a healthy vine pulsating with necessary nutrients gathered from soil, water, and sun, Jesus is full of life. Everything you and I need to be fully alive and *flourishing* is available in Jesus. He is the vine; we are the branches. Secondly, we are made to be fruitful. Unlike inanimate stones that just sit on the ground, you are created to be fruitful and to multiply, having the character of the vine—Jesus—show up in you and through you for the blessing of those around you. Grapes dangling on the end of a branch are the product of the vine, not the branch. The branch is fruitful, not because the branch produces anything, but because the branch is a healthy conduit for the vine. By the Holy Spirit, Jesus continues

**to live *His* life
in *His* world
through *His* disciples.**

Which means, third, our role in the *fruit* process is to remain connected to Jesus. If you focus on fruit-production—doing what you think Jesus wants on your own wisdom and power—you will tire quickly and feel barren. If, however, you focus on *abiding*, cultivating your relational connection to King Jesus through His Spirit, you will find His spiritual life pulsing through you, producing abundant fruit. In addition to loving God as Father, a central priority for you as a growing, multiplying disciple is developing your personal, intimate relationship with King Jesus, through the Holy Spirit. What will it take for you to adjust your fast-paced, always *on*, jam-filled life so that this can happen more intentionally?

Remember, as Paul says in Galatians 5:22-23: the *joyful, peace*-making *love* of Christ that is *patient* with the annoying, *kind* with the rude, *good* to the hurtful, *gentle* with the harsh, and *faithfully self-controlled* when tempted to be otherwise...*that* love is the fruit of the Holy Spirit in your life. It is not yours to anxiously produce. Invite the Spirit to bear the fruit of love, so that the same love that *found* you, might now be found by others *through* you. Follow the Holy Spirit into a fruitful life.

"Thank You for the privilege of partnering with my Christian siblings for this season of spiritual growth.

Form Yourself in us Jesus, as we pray daily for one another.

Give us Your pursuing heart for those we love, work with, and live near.

Equip and inspire us to disciple with others who will multiply."

7

DISCIPLE

together to Multiply

Partnership – Prayer – Transformation – Multiplication

INTRODUCTION

In the 2008 Summer Olympics in Beijing, China something happened to our U.S. track team that had never happened before. It was painful to watch. In the span of just 30 minutes, both our men's and women's 4X100 relay teams, heavily favored to win gold, came up empty-handed. They didn't even medal because they didn't finish. There are two critical components to relays: being fast—and we were world class fast—and passing the baton.

The fate of the whole team rests in 3 hand-offs. And ironically, in both races at the very same point in the race, with the U.S. in the lead, the *final* exchange failed. The baton dropped to the ground and with it four years of intense training and hopes of Olympic glory. It was especially difficult for *Lauren Williams* since she had dropped the same baton 4 years earlier in Athens. Can you imagine? Both teams were quick as lightening, but it all fizzled when the hand-off never happened.

That hand-off is *so* important.

This is true in the Christian life as well. God's plan to redeem the world rests on an *exchange*. One person—Jesus—helps a few grow in their faith, who in turn help a few grow in their faith. And on and on it goes. The Gospel baton is received and passed forward. If you're a disciple of Jesus, it is because this intentional process of one person sharing the gospel with another and then with another made its way down the track…to you. Who was it?

Who *introduced* you to Jesus?

Who helped you grow? Aren't you glad they did? Aren't you glad they took the time to pour into you? We all have a spiritual heritage. Somebody discipled the person who discipled you. Just like our great grandparents birthed our grandparents who birthed our parents, who birthed us, so, too, our *spiritual lineage* is traced all the way back—person to person to person, eventually to Jesus. He invested His life in a few—like Peter, James and John—and they caught the vision together that they were to intentionally disciple others who would intentionally disciple still others.

Jesus is like a rock His Father tossed into the water of this world, and whose ripple effect is still making waves! If you're a disciple of Jesus, that ripple made its way to you. It wants to make its way *through* you into the lives of others who will grow and mature, and then pass it on to still others.

This is God's *design.*

This is His singular strategy for reaching men, women, and children—like us—from all nations. One life—Jesus—multiplied into millions; not simply by adding one life at a time, but preparing new disciples to reproduce reproducers. From the very beginning, Jesus' way of making disciples wasn't addition; it was *multiplication.*

If you're a homeowner, and in particular if you take pride in your lawn, you understand this—*negatively* with dandelions, but *positively* with those little seeds that line the top of grass stems in the Spring. One stem produces a bunch of seeds that fall to the ground and *multiply* into many stems of grass, which grow and reproduce seed that falls and multiplies. And this process just keeps going. Eventually you get a thick yard.

This is how Jesus *disciples* **the nations.**

As the initial stem, He produced the initial disciples. He *invested* in them intentionally, *prayed* for them daily, *lived* life with them— laughing, crying, playing, coaching, teaching, encouraging, challenging...etc. Jesus' very life was multiplied into the lives of His disciples so that their lives could be multiplied into many others. And by God's grace that process made its way to us. Other disciples have come alongside us to water us and tend to us (and we them in a mutual way); mending us where we're broken, gently but boldly pruning us so that we can flourish even more. And they've done that for us that we might do that for others. That *we* might prepare each other to do that with still others. That's how you get multiplication.

Are you *catching* this vision?

The heart of what it means to be a disciple of Jesus is playing your part in helping other disciples follow Jesus who will help still other disciples do the same. As the Apostle Paul says, *"What you have heard from me...entrust to faithful men who will be able to teach others."* (2 Timothy 2:2). That's the original 4G network! Four generations of disciples:

Jesus to Paul,
Paul to Timothy,
Timothy to faithful men,
faithful men discipling still others.

This is how the Gospel baton is passed well.

Sadly, the vast majority of Christians have never experienced what Paul describes. Many of us attend church and listen to sermons — maybe even fellowship in a small group — but personally discipling with each another is very rare. And we desperately need it. Your interest in reading and applying this book suggests that you are aware that spiritual growth is not an end in and of itself; it is a means to the end of reproducing and helping others grow.

I wonder who you will disciple with *next*?

Are you beginning to pray about that?

Being a disciple of Jesus is a lot like a race. Less like a sprint and more like a relay. However, you're not trying to *beat* the people running next to you; you're actually trying to help them finish the race. God has given us to each other to help us run our leg well and to help each other get the Gospel baton in the hands of others who will do the same. We are given to each other to disciple together in order to multiply. Jesus' 2000 year-old strategy is *still* changing the world: Disciple together…to multiply. Let's do this.

PARTNERSHIP

What is it about January 1st? Something in us loves new beginnings, fresh starts, and clean slates. As we flip the calendar into a new year it is common for us to develop novel commitments. How many resolutions can one actually make and break in a lifetime? I must laugh at myself or I'll cry as I analyze my paltry track record. Whether it's a diet to lose weight, a renewed commitment to get to bed at an earlier hour, or a journey through the Bible that often stalls out in Deuteronomy, we are better at identifying what *needs* to be changed and what "better" looks like, than we are at following through. Change is a stubborn challenge because we are creatures of habit, and old habits do in fact die hard.

I remember one December as I was approaching a new year, I asked a personal trainer for a customized daily regimen that I could begin after the holidays. (Come to think of it, maybe it is the gluttony of the holidays that justifies our improbable, lofty January goals.) I was quite eager for guidance and I assumed my teachable spirit would be met with great enthusiasm. I was sadly mistaken. He simply smiled at me and said, *"Stephen, you can get your body in shape (that's the good news), but having a program will not help you get there unless you identify someone with whom you can do it. Get a partner and I'll give you your plan."* I did not see that coming.

**I needed a some*one*,
not a some*thing*.**

As years have passed this wise counsel has held true in the area of physical fitness, and it is equally true when it comes to our spiritual fitness.

Most of our best-intentioned plans fail, not because we pursue wrong things, but because we pursue them in *isolation*. All too easily we convince ourselves that growth is a private enterprise. It would be, if God had set it up that way. As it turns out, personal growth and maturity is largely the fruit of an intentional covenant relationship where two or three commit to invest their lives in each other, seeing each other to the finish-line of faithfulness. Truth is, my own motivation for change often wanes, either when the going gets tough or the positive results grow scarce. In those moments my "resolutions" become fragile. I often assuage my own disappointment by remembering that I was only pursuing "better" anyway, and there's no shame in stopping because my new goal wasn't revealed to anyone. The secret is safe with me. But honestly, real satisfaction doesn't come through justifying our failure; it comes through experiencing transformation! And for that, I have come to believe that it is critical that we partner with a few others for a season of intentional development. They play a critical role in my maturity and I in theirs. We are a mutual blessing to one another.

And that's exactly how God *designed* it to be,
and how Jesus *modeled* it.

In the Gospels, while we do find Jesus performing miracles among the masses and teaching the crowds biblical content, His modeling of the specifics of a life lived for God was reserved for a few. The twelve disciples certainly had greater access to Jesus than the crowds, but actually it was Peter, James, and John who received

His most personal investment. Jesus deliberately and unashamedly gathered the three around Him, knowing that the greatest transformation comes through an intimate exchange of persons.

**For iron to sharpen iron
the two blades must** *engage.*

And so it is with spiritual growth. The intimacy and positive friction of a single life engaging another, or a few, sharpens the dulled hearts and hones the focus of the participants. Jesus was willing to risk being misunderstood. He gave exclusive time to the Three so that they could imitate Him and model His life with others. Jesus took a long view of reaching the world. Rather than trying to quickly mass-produce disciples though an attractively marketed event or program, Jesus chose the slow methodical approach of intentional relationships, believing that they had the greatest potential for lasting impact. He must have been onto something since you and I are interested in discipling with a few others over 2000 years later.

Jesus' method wasn't lost on the Apostle Paul. Like Jesus, Paul gladly seized opportunities to preach and teach large gatherings, but also, like Jesus, the heart and soul of his ministry was partnering with a few for an intentional season of growth. Whether it was Priscilla and Acquila, Barnabus and John Mark, or Silas and Timothy, Paul embraced the strategy of discipling with a few for the purpose of eventual multiplication. In fact, it is how he birthed churches and encouraged churches to grow into maturity. We see this clearly affirmed in the first chapter of his letter to Jesus' disciples in Thessalonica. Paul offers at least five key ingredients worthy of our emulation.

Spiritual growth happens as we
gently nurture **one another.**

Paul employs the image of a nursing mother who willingly sets aside her tasks for the sake of her child's care and development. This takes sacrifice, but those growing alongside of you are worth it. They believe you're worth it! Secondly, spiritual growth is the fruit of

giving **one another** *access* **to our lives.**

Paul explains that, due to his growing affection, he was not only eager to share the Gospel with them, but his *own life* as well. When the opening of God's Word *combines* with the vulnerable opening of one's heart the journey is ripe for mutual growth. When we hold back, the exercise becomes purely academic. When we do life together, learning becomes practical and catchable.

A third ingredient that makes an intentional discipling relationship a fertile context for growth is

modeling godliness **for one another.**

Larger group experiences are good for broadly consuming content, but it takes the intimacy of a few to directly experience growing godliness in specific arenas of life. When we're close and committed and regular, we can be eye-witnesses of Christ's formation in each other's lives, which spurs us on to pursue the same.

A fourth ingredient for spiritual growth is

challenging **one another.**

Through words of encouragement when we want to give up and words of exhortation when we're veering off course, we can—like a father to a child—challenge one another to walk the path of faithfulness. We need challenge but we are leery of receiving it from near strangers.

Finally, while we hear God's voice directly through Scripture and through the promptings of His Spirit within us, He also intends for us to

hear Him *through* **one another.**

I recommend a covenant partnership, like a Triad, where three men or three women enter into a mutually edifying and equipping spiritual journey for a year or so. These small, same gender, intentional relationships can provide a significant context for spiritual growth. The true benefits of a Triad, however, depend upon the degree to which each member gives the others permission to speak grace and truth as they are led. As we listen to God in prayer for one another, we have the unique privilege of speaking into each other's lives. Are you experiencing this? If so, give God thanks and take a moment this week to let those discipling with you know how grateful you are for their partnership in the Gospel. And if not, your journey together probably needs some course correction. Just another chance to be real and to extend and receive grace. There's always grace.

PRAYER

It was a beautiful sunny day under a deep blue Colorado sky. I was leading a group of high school seniors on a white-water rafting trip down the Arkansas River. Well, when I say "leading," I was in charge of their well-being on the trip, but on the water we were in the hands of an abled guide. The trek through the rapids went off without a hitch. That is, until we came to the last one. It was so precarious we had to pull over and climb up to an overlook, where the guide coached us on how we would navigate it. I have to laugh as I think back to his directions. They weren't wrong or unclear; we were just complete novices and teenage boys don't have a great track-record of good listening skills. As we got back into the raft I knew we were doomed.

His last piece of advice was a source of encouragement and discouragement at the same time. After giving us the three keys to successively traversing this monstrous, churning torrent of white foam, he alerted us to the grave danger of the rapid immediately following were we to dump and float on by ourselves. I was ready to pull the plug at the word "grave." The boys, however, were adamant that we conquer the beast. Our guide soothed my concerns only slightly by pointing out the *spotters* on the bank of the river. Like life-guards, they stood ready to throw red bags filled with yellow rope toward flailing rafters. If that were to be us—and it seemed like fate—we were coached to raise one hand into the air wide open and pray that a rope would land in it. Again, encouraging and discouraging at the same time. What are the chances of *that* happening?

Well, with caution to the wind, we bravely set sail...only to embrace our demise within moments. I remember hearing the sigh of the guide behind me as we failed to employ his strategy. He knew we were toast. We plunged down into the fierce wall of water and everyone shot straight up flying skyward. While submerged in a million bubbles, I remembered the ambitious and crazy wisdom of opening my hand and raising it high. As I breeched the surface, that's what I did. And I kid you not, within three seconds I saw a long yellow rope cutting the air, making for my hand like it was on a personal mission.

**The odds obviously were not good,
but the throw *was*!**

It hit my palm and I grabbed on, and relief washed over me as I was pulled with strength to the bank. I rested as I clung to a large rock. Once I gathered myself I climbed out and sought the spotter at the end of the rope. It was a young lady. *"How in the world did you do that?,"* I asked with gratitude. She smiled, *"Had my eye on you the whole time. I was just hoping you were lookin' for the rope."*

Though she was unaware, that college student taught me a valuable lesson that day: we all need personal spotters on our journey into multiplication. Life is unpredictable at best and dangerous at worst, and we all need people in our lives who have their eye on us, who are ready and willing to intervene on our behalf. She was no help to me in the rapid, but she was tracking me because she cared. She was aware of my need and ready to play her part in carrying me to safety.

**One of the best ways we do this for
each other is through *prayer*.**

We don't even have to be in the same city. As long as we are personally connected and current with each other, we can spot each other by carrying one another out of the rapids to the Rock—that is Jesus—through prayer. And as my hand had to be open that day to receive the rope, prayer works best when our hearts are open to one another to receive its ministry.

This is why our intentional investment in each other is so important. As we journey together—opening our lives to one another—our capacity to effectively spot one another grows. We're able to thank God daily for the joys *and* the challenges because we know that God is at work. We are able to thank God for the spiritual growth we're seeing in our siblings' lives and we can ask God for more. It is certainly a bit of a mystery, but through prayer we are actually able to play a part in the formation of Jesus in each other's lives.

The apostle Paul *certainly* **thought so.**

Over and over again we find him beginning his New Testament letters to young, growing disciples just like us with words of affirmation and prayer. He was their spiritual spotter. His eye was on them. His affection was great for them. *"I hold you in my heart for you are all partakers with me of grace...I yearn for you all with the affection of Christ Jesus"* (Philippians 1:7-8). This is why it was his literal joy to pray for them: *"I thank my God in all my remembrance of you, always in every prayer of mine for you all making my prayer with joy, because of your partnership in the gospel"* (Philippians 1:3-5). Though in prison, unable to be with them in person, Paul was eager to be with them in spirit. His confidence in God was so great that he believed the same God living in him was able to accomplish great things in them. And so he prayed that their

> *"love may abound more and more..*
> *and so be pure and blameless...*
> *and be filled with the fruit of righteousness*
> *that comes through Jesus Christ, to the glory and praise of God."*
> (Philippians 1:9-11)

He didn't pray for them out of duty. He wasn't skeptical about the outcome. He prayed with confident delight, leaving the results in the hands of God. And we have the distinct privilege of doing the same with one another. Every day. Or as faithfully as God leads. It's never about checking the box. It's always about growing the fellowship. As you know, some parts of the river are calmer than others. But no matter, each stage of the journey is an opportunity to have our eye on one another; carrying each other to Jesus. I was always struck as a boy by the story of the men who carried their paralyzed friend to Jesus, lowering him down through a hole they literally dug in the roof. That's commitment. And that's prayer. They knew his need and they knew the Provider.

Our prayers for one another *link* **the two.**

Are your prayers for those with whom you are discipling getting more specific? Are you spotting one another? Are you opening your hearts to one another—sharing requests and receiving the wonderful ministry of prayer? Can you imagine the growth and transformation that we might witness in the Church if everyone had a few spotters carrying them to Jesus every day? Wow! Join me in praying even now that it would be so.

TRANSFORMATION

Think back to when you were a kid. What toys did you enjoy playing with most? As a father of seven—and a kid at heart—I've had many opportunities to witness the early years of play. (I have a garage full of ex-toys!) What is striking to me is that a common theme for both girls and boys is what we might call "creative change." My girls have always enjoyed taking plain paper, tape, glue and glitter, and creating a craft. Something new and beautiful from ordinary stuff. Similarly, I'd often find them lining up their dolls, putting on their cute little outfits, acting like one is the mom and the other is the daughter. Amazing how a plain plastic doll can come to life in their hands. As they aged they began to see each other as the dolls. Playing "dress-up" became fashionable. For a few hours they'd set aside their normal clothes and don shinny, sequined gowns, becoming the princesses they long to be. "Creative change" leads to lots of giggles.

This is true of the toys that little boys like as well. Did you ever pop out little plastic parts and assemble them into red Ferraris or silver WWII bombers with decals? Or, how about Legos? You could have a multi-colored pile of nothin' and thirty minutes later you're running through the house with a rocket ship…that you made! One of a kind. And then somebody invented my favorite childhood toy—Transformers. Cool looking metallic robots could morph in seconds into trucks and pterodactyls and guns. What looked like a simple tape-deck could evolve with a few twists into a fierce fighting machine with missile launchers for arms. That's Transformers—"creative change" in the palm of your hand. Kids love that kind of change. It's what makes "Play-Doh" such a perennial winner across the gender spectrum. A common lump of blue clay-like material becomes a sail boat or a snake or a hammer in a flash, and then something else in another. So much of our play early on is about *change*.

And we really never *outgrow* that.

Think about the entertainment we consume as adults. Isn't it just a grown up version of the creative change we've always loved? We spend billions on movies as ordinary men and women assume roles and develop characters with whom we fall in love. Many of the popular video games have the accumulation of assets and building materials and the construction of forts and cities at their core. Plain country sides become vast kingdoms worth protecting. We listen to music that artists create with new beats, new chord progressions, fresh takes on life and love and heartache. We take and edit pictures with our phones and then post them for the world to see.

Creative *change.*

Think about our love of sports. We're mesmerized by athletes who train their frames and hone their skills to do amazing things under the greatest of pressure. Whether it's throwing or hitting something further or harder or more accurately, athletes grow up before our eyes—little girls and boys become bigger than life, doing things we could only dream of doing. Some of us spend hours watching cooking shows as renowned chefs turn unrelated raw materials into delectable cuisine. Nature shows intrigue us as they reveal the metamorphosis that takes place in plants and animals every day right under our noses. Just think of the mysterious wonder of a butterfly. It's all about creative change. That's what enthralls us. There something about it that speaks to the very core of who we are. But what is it?

Might we be fascinated *by* creative change because we're made *for* creative change ourselves? Your own body has naturally grown and developed; might the internal you be made to do the same? I think so. Unlike inanimate objects, we are living beings made to become more and more like the One who made us.

You are made for *spiritual* **metamorphosis.**

Jesus is eager to get busy at the molecular level of your soul—transforming you from the inside out. Creative change. By His Spirit He matures His own to become more like Him. As the apostle Paul explains: *"...beholding the glory of the Lord, we all are being transformed into the same image from one degree of glory to another"* (2 Corinthians 3:18). In other words, there is a glorious version of you! Have you ever thought of it that way? *"A glorious version of me?"*

All too easily we reduce the Christian life to rule-following and box-checking that essentially bides the time until we pass. *That* is not the plan. You are made for far more. King Jesus didn't die and rise simply to secure your eternal destiny (of course He *did* do that!). He now reigns to transform you into the glory for which you were uniquely made. And He doesn't start from scratch. He doesn't scrap you and start over. He gently and ably takes your raw materials—your history (the good, the bad, and the ugly), your personality, your mind, your training, your passions, your dreams...etc. He takes *you* as His grace finds you, and He molds and shapes you into His image. *"He (God) predestined us to be conformed to the image of His Son, in order that He (Jesus) might be the firstborn among many brothers (and sisters)"* (Romans 8:29).

It's all about *family* resemblance.

Again, in Galatians 4:19, Paul expresses his great desire for young disciples: *"my little children, for whom I am again in the anguish of childbirth until Christ is formed in you!"* Spiritual metamorphosis is not the replacement of you with Christ, but the arrival of Christ *in* you and the revealing of Christ *through* you. Therefore, His pursuit through you (of those you love and work with and live near) will look uniquely different than His pursuit through anyone else. And yet, both will share His fingerprints. This is what "Christian" means—*little Christ*. Each of us becoming unique miniature versions of Jesus. This is the way the whole earth will literally be filled with His glory! Through us. The world has seen Jesus, but the world has never seen Him through someone like you.

You offer an *exceptional* expression of Christ.

And *that* is an amazing thought.

Now, we do have a part to play in this transformation. It's a bit of a mystery but since God equips us with wills, we can't sit idly by and expect creative change to just...*happen*. God always does the work, but   He's chosen to work in and through *our* will to bring about *His*. The earlier allusion to dress-ups may prove helpful at this point. Paul says in Ephesians 4:22-24, *"put off your old self, which belongs to your former manner of life...and be renewed in the spirit of your minds, and put on the new self, created after the likeness of God in true righteousness and holiness."* It's not so much the removal of you as a person, but the daily intentional discarding of the old patterns of sin and selfishness and the growing embrace of the righteous character of Christ—inviting Him to live His life through you. A new rhythm.

Put *off*, **put** *on*.
Put *off*, **put** *on*.

Old shabby clothes may feel familiar and comfortable, but if they are not aligned with Jesus they have to go in order to make room for new clothes. Don't you long to be renewed, to be newly created after the likeness of God Himself? On your own this is impossible. With Christ alive within you this is happening even now. Invite it to happen even more. Creative change. You're made for this!

MULTIPLICATION

In college I remember an economics professor posing this question: *"If I were to offer you one million dollars today or one penny, promising to double your money every day for the next 30 days, which would you take?"* Though it felt like a set-up, where the most advantageous answer was probably the least attractive—the penny plan—I couldn't resist becoming an instant millionaire. I also couldn't imagine the penny plan amounting to anything remotely close to a million dollars. As it turns out, I'd only have earned $163.84 by day 15. But by day 30, I would have netted $5.4 million. So, which is a better deal? One million today, or 5.4 million in 30 days? It's a rather dramatic illustration of the mind-boggling difference *multiplication* makes and the fruitful benefit of delayed gratification. $1x2x2x2x2...etc. eventually yields 5.4 million dollars. This is similar to the logic behind the familiar adage that it's better to teach a man *how* to fish than it is to give a man a fish to eat in one sitting. Fill him for a meal or feed him for a lifetime. It's the difference between addition and multiplication.

And this *distinction* plays out as disciples of Jesus too.

If we assume that only some of us are called to pursue and make new disciples, the Church's growth will be slow and incremental, and we will always be one generation away from extinction. If, however, everyone who receives Gospel grace also embraces the call of Jesus to make new disciples (or to help existing ones catch the vision for multiplication) then the Church's growth will be exponential—an unstoppable presence wherever the Gospel is found. I am introducing this journey because of the conviction that every disciple *is* called to multiply.

This pattern of birth, growth, and multiplication is inherent to the human experience. My grandparents only had two sons. Those two sons, however, had five children each and the third generation is 52 strong. How proud my "Papa" and "Nana" would be! In the same way, the life of a disciple of Jesus is intended to bear fruit, fruit that will ultimately grow up and bear fruit of its own. I mentioned dandelions in the introduction to this life-long priority. Those lovely, but pesky little yard trolls. Isn't it amazing how some yards are filled with them, while others have none? It's not that some weeds choose to multiply while others don't. It's that yards without dandelions stay that way because it takes dandelion seeds to get more. Yards that have even just one will predictably have more the next year as dandelions inevitably seed many more times beyond themselves. Multiplication is in their DNA. It's what they were made to do. They root, they grow, they shine, and then they multiply.

That **is to be true of us as well.**

You see this profoundly in the apostle Paul's relationship with Timothy. By God's providence, Timothy learned of grace through his mother Eunice, who discovered grace through her mother Lois. That's multiply. Someone entrusted the Gospel to Lois and she passed it on. Paul draws alongside Timothy and encourages him to do the same: *"Follow the pattern of the sound words that you have heard from me...by the Holy Spirit who dwells within us, guard the good deposit entrusted to you"* (2 Timothy 1:13). Guard it, but don't conceal it. It bears repeating, *"what you have heard from me...entrust to faithful men who be able to teach others also"* (2 Timothy 2:2). This intentional process involves discipling together...in order to multiply. Being rooted in grace, growing up, shining, and then multiplying.

As Gospel grace saturates the deepest parts of your soul, it begins to well back up within you and make its way out. You can hardly contain it. The good news is like a fountain, we weren't made to contain it; we were made to share it. You were made to have the life of Jesus reproduced within you, and then to have the life-of-Jesus-in-you reproduced in the lives of those around you. In some cases, this will mean pursuing those who are outside the faith but inside your reach with grace and truth and kindness. In other cases, it will mean embarking on an extended journey with an eager disciple, helping that person grow in the priorities of *Multiply*. Either way, once you're rooted in grace, you grow and shine, and then help others do the same.

If you are working through this book with a few other disciples, it is time to begin preparing for your next journey with a few more. My experience with most "studies" or small groups is that they often have an unspoken *perpetual* covenant. Though it may lose a few along the way, barring any unforeseen conflict, the group stays together indefinitely. For the most part, the outward mission of pursuing others to fold them in slips off the radar as the group becomes a bit ingrown. Frankly, just the thought of not being together strikes fear in the hearts of most participants. I know. I get it. I love being linked deeply with the two guys in my Triad as I write this.

**Finding a soul-companion is a *gift*
none of us wants to lose.**

My sincere hope and expectation is that you won't...lose. You *will* multiply, but you won't lose the deepened relationships forged through intentional discipleship. The core of this journey into multiplication is an intimate relational exchange. It's not simply acquiring new information. It's processing life together before God and witnessing God's profound work of grace in each other's lives. You don't just move on from that. My encouragement would be to consider how you might maintain some semblance of these important relationships over the next year or so. Get creative with it. Perhaps you decide to meet for breakfast or lunch once a month to check in and seek each other's counsel as you disciple with a few others. Maybe you seize a portion of Sunday morning to connect and pray so that the rest of your schedule is free to multiply. Or maybe, as you multiply into three new Triads, you will have quarterly experiences where you draw the "extended family" together, the nine of you, for sharing and prayer. This could prove to be a great source of encouragement to all as each one senses they are part of something bigger. A kingdom movement actually.

For God so loved the world that He sent His only Son *into* the world. His Son—Jesus—so loved the world that He gave His life *for* the world. But before He did, the Son poured His life into a Triad— Peter, James, and John—investing in them and modeling for them what it meant to be truly human. After Jesus' resurrection, the Father and the Son poured out the Holy Spirit into the lives of the first disciples, and they multiplied. They pursued men, women, and children with Gospel grace and folded them into the Kingdom.

And that *wave of grace* has made its way to us.

Now it's our turn. You don't have to be an expert. You just have to be available. Who has God been placing on your heart, with whom you might disciple in order to multiply? You might even ask them now to pray about joining you. It's a joy to be invited into such an adventure. Oh, that God has included us in this glorious endeavor. Real fruit. Fruit that will last!

LINK
deeply with a Few

DISCIPLE
together to Multiply

INVEST
in the Church

"Thank You for the joy of being a part of my church.

Everything I have belongs to You!

Help me to cheerfully and generously invest my
time and skills, money and possessions
for the spiritual maturity and Kingdom impact of my
church."

8

INVEST

in the Church

Organism – Stewardship – Generosity – Pleasure

INTRODUCTION

One of my favorite childhood memories was coming home on a cold winter evening to the smell of my mom's vegetable soup. We'd often have a roast on Sunday and then for Tuesday's dinner she'd combine the left-overs with potatoes, corn, beans, carrots, diced tomatoes, and some kind of wonderful broth. It was so good! I think she even snuck some lima beans in there (which was fine as long as they were in the soup). Now, what might my mom's soup have in common with say...the Boston Pops, the human shoulder, and a football team? Well, in each case,

the *whole* is greater
than the *sum* of the parts.

Imagine eating a handful of corn and lima beans, and then washing it down with beef broth and a diced tomato. No thank you. But throw it all into a boiling pot...*delicious*.

Likewise, while I love to listen to string instruments, I am not as big a fan of brass. And a drum all by itself is great for a solo interlude at a rock concert, but not so great for an hour by itself in the bedroom. Now, assemble them all together and it's a symphony. Literally. "Sym—phony" means "together sound"! Harmony. I'll give up a night to take in a symphony.

The same is true with a football team. The star running back and wide receiver may be amazing talents, but you couldn't field a championship team with 25 of each. In order to win in the NFL you need to have a fair amount of 6-foot-6 linemen, a bunch of fast, tough linebackers, and even a five-foot-nothin'-kicker. Even a little shoulder is a complex joint made up of three bones, nine major muscles, and a whole host of fibrous ligaments. I injured my right one trying to throw out a guy at third base from center field. It took almost two years to heal. (And I didn't get him out!)

Every *part* matters
to the health of the *whole*.

Soup, symphonies, sports, shoulders. All around us there are everyday examples where the whole is greater than the sum of the parts. If you were to lay out each part of my shoulder on a table, what use would it be? But when you organize, when you coordinate the various pieces into a joint it can lift *eight times* its own weight! That's pretty amazing. Some things are just better together. Sounds like a Reese's commercial.

The same is true of the *Church*.

In America, we've gotten used to saying that we "go to church," as if it's a place. Or, we'll ask somebody, "Where do you attend?" Again, a place. And of course every gathered Church has an address, but we don't find physical structures described in the New Testament. What we *do* find are descriptions of a people—a family. It's not so much "where" as "who." Sons and daughters of the same Father, brothers and sisters sharing a relationship with King Jesus, united by Gospel grace, having the same Holy Spirit, committed to link deeply and to disciple together with the goal of multiplication—pursuing and restoring those who are outside the faith, but inside our reach. The Church isn't a place, it's a movement of people—united, growing, multiplying into the lives of others.

Over and over, the New Testament teaches us that the whole of us is greater than the sum of our parts. We function at our greatest capacity as a people when we're all in...*together.* *"When each part is working properly the Body grows so that it builds itself up in love"* (Ephesians 4:16). Or again, in 1 Corinthians 12:4-7, *"God empowers a variety of gifts, services, and activities in everyone. Each one is given the manifestation of the Spirit for the common good."* We are gifted by God for the sake of others. That is a revolutionary concept.

In the Christian life, we do have a *personal* relationship with Jesus, but we were never intended to maintain a *private* one. We were meant to pool the resources God has graciously entrusted to each of us so that He might accomplish more among us and through us than He could by ourselves. It takes the abiding unity and growing maturity of the constituent parts to make a family whole and healthy and fruitful. And the same is true with the human body.

Each individual part's usefulness depends upon it being vitally connected and committed to the rest of the parts. Pull them all together and the body can grow and learn and move and impact those around it. And this is God's vision

**for the *global* Church
and for each *local* expression of it.**

After saving us individually, God could have left us to journey with Him alone. In addition to our personal walk, however, we have a life together—a role to play in the spiritual maturity and Kingdom impact of the local church to which we're committed. With the resources my wife and I invest in our church—time, skills, energy, and money—we could make a small contribution to God's work in His world *by ourselves*. When you combine our investment, however, with all of the investments that each person generously makes, the potential impact increases exponentially.

And this is *by design*.

Now, for a variety of reasons some of us have convinced ourselves we can live without the local church. Sadly for some, the experience has been painful. The church—forgiven *sinners*—certainly can be messy relationally, with extensive collateral damage. Others of us feel unfulfilled. For whatever reason, the church is failing to satisfy our particular longings (perhaps we expect too much). Others of us simply find the unpredictability of relationships unnerving. While still others are just not persuaded they have anything of value to contribute. Many of us choose to disengage for these reasons and more: wounds, selfishness, control, inadequacy...etc.

We need a fresh vision!

According to Scripture, being a part of the Church is not only required for Jesus' disciples, it's a central part of the journey—and one of God's greatest gifts. In the Father's sovereign plan He employs our aches and disappointments to draw us to Himself; He lovingly reminds us that it isn't all about us anyway. He challenges our self-sufficiency through the gifts and service of others, and He graciously equips us by His Spirit to have something unique to invest.

What is your current relationship with your local church? Are you an integral part of the whole? If not, what holds you back? Every single piece matters. We need carrots and potatoes, clarinets and cellos, cornerbacks and running backs, scapulae and deltoids. We need them all. And the church needs you. And we need each other. How compelling and beautiful and fruitful could your local church be if every single member became truly *invested*? Let's learn together what this might look like.

ORGANISM

The variety of living species in our world offers clear reminders of the matchless creativity of God. Some are microscopic, some too vast to calculate. *All* are unique. Consider, for example, *size*. Did you know that you can line up over 20 million of the average virus side-by-side...in just one inch? Yuck! Contrast this with the Blue Whale—the largest mammal in the world—whose lengths can exceed 100 feet and are known to weigh over 200 tons. How about *height*? The tallest man—Robert Wadlow—stood at eight feet, 11 inches. His massive frame, however, is dwarfed by *Hyperion* a coastal Redwood from northern California with a verified height of 379 feet—nine stories taller than the *Statue of Liberty*. That's a living plant from a small seed, producing enough wood to frame out 12 two-story American homes. Amazing! *Speed*? Cheetahs have been clocked at 75 mph and are able to accelerate from zero to 60 in just three seconds. Ants on the other hand, can only move at about .18 mph (over 400 times slower than Cheetahs!) but are strong enough to carry over 50 times their body weight and can close their jaws at speeds of 140 mph with a force 500 times their body mass.

Living organisms are *truly* inspiring.

Perhaps one of the most unsung in all creation is the *Aspen* tree. The landscape of my home away from home, Colorado, is dotted throughout with massive aspen groves. The contrast of their light, airy delicate green leaves with the prickly, tough needles of the blue spruce is indeed a spectacle. The aspen's beauty above the ground is perhaps only exceeded by the masterful complexity of their life just beneath it. Aspen groves maintain a secret in the soil that is the "root" of their success.

When you see a grove of aspen your eyes may take in thousands of individual trees, but in reality you're only looking at a single, living organism. Below, one root stem stretches itself horizontally, rooting itself periodically, sending a *ramet* vertically to the soil. That ramet becomes a shoot and then a new tree trunk which can reach upwards to 100-feet. In time, that new trunk sends out its own root stems from which new ramets are born. So a grove of aspen can be massive (50+ acres!), yet the trees on the two extremes will be genetically identical. If we're anointing a champion for size and weight, the aspen grove would be unrivaled. And like the redwood, it's just a plant born of a small seed.

But born to live and *thrive.*

Aspen are born to grow and multiply. Of all the living organisms in the world, they are perhaps only outclassed by one: the Christian Church!

The Greek New Testament word for *church* means "assembly" or "gathering," and it finds both local and global expression. Locally, in cities and towns, each individual gathering of disciples of King Jesus (*a* church) offers a tangible, *visible* manifestation of His Kingdom—God's people yielded to God's reign. These unique Kingdom-outposts combine with others to create an *invisible* world-wide network (*the* Church). Thousands of individual churches form one living organism united by their common reception of Gospel grace and common mission of pursuing future disciples. The same is true of a local church. While some may have 50, 1000, or 20,000 individuals, just like an aspen grove, they are one united people. They are one living organism, sharing the same root, which is King Jesus and whose "genes" are reproduced in the life of each disciple and each church.

In order to capture this concept of the church (many disciples, one living organism) the apostle Paul chose the human frame as his primary analogy. In addition to being the quintessential living organism, the human body is a magnificent, animated example of how the whole is far greater than the sum of the parts. My thumb is of no use apart from my fingers, but together my hand can be very productive. So also, each individual disciple, left to his/her independent self, is of little use in the Kingdom, but when combined with other "fingers" (disciples) there's no limit to the difference joined disciples can make.

But it's *more* than that.

For Paul, the human body is not merely a good *analogy*. Perhaps his most radical insight is that the assembled disciples (the local church) are in fact the present physical manifestation of the resurrected King Jesus Himself. In Ephesians 1:22-23 he explains that, *"He* (God the Father) *gave Him* (Jesus) *as head of all things to the church, which is His body."* Or, *"...we are members of His body."* Similarly, in 1 Corinthians 12:27 Paul declares: *"Now you are the body of Christ and individually members of it."* Or, *"For just as the body* (human) *is one and has many members...so it is with Christ"* (1 Corinthians 12:12). Now, we expect him to say "the Church", but Paul understands the church to be the real, living, breathing earthly expression of the now risen, reigning King of glory. Let me say that again (and ask yourself if you really believe it about your church): *the church is the real, living, breathing earthly expression of the now risen, reigning King of glory.* As if Jesus still has hands and feet, and a heart and a voice...through us!

The implications are *profound.*

Thumbs and ears and patellar tendons have necessary, particular roles to play in the meaningful functionality of the body. So also, each individual disciple of Jesus has a *particular role* to play in the health and Kingdom vitality of the local living organism— the church. In other words, by the Holy Spirit, King Jesus intends for each gathering of disciples (our churches) to serve as a unique expression of His life and reign in our particular communities.

Which is a far, far cry from seeing the church as a building in which one attends a worship service...periodically. Oh, that King Jesus might renew our *vision* and *commitment* to Him and each other!

If we are to get there, we have to overcome two primary barriers. First, we have to stop basing our connection to a local church on *personal preference* alone. While it is certainly acceptable to take a season to discern whether or not you "fit" (or better, are being called) into a particular local expression of the King, it is *not* acceptable to simply decide that you don't and to check out completely, or to flit from one "grove" to another as if your long-term investment is optional or unnecessary. Some aspens in a grove are near a water source and gladly supply water to the parts of the organism that are furthest away.

Imagine if they simply *chose* not to.

As hard as it is for self-inclined, self-sufficient Americans to settle into community, we all must accept that Gospel grace comes with the high calling of playing our integral role in the growth and impact of the whole. *"God arranged the members in the body, each one of them, as He chose. God has so composed the body...that the members may have the same care for one another"* (1 Corinthians 18, 24-25). This is either an impossible pipedream or a reality we must all quickly embrace.

Which leads to a second barrier:
feeling inadequate.

It is one thing to become theologically convinced that we're part of the body of Christ. It is another thing to be persuaded of our role's *importance*. We're naturally a comparative people. We assess certain physical traits as being more desirous than others and sadly we do this with spiritual roles of ministry as well. Paul confronts this with down- to-earth common sense in: *"The body does not consist of one member but of many. If the whole body were an eye, where would be the sense of hearing? If the whole body were an ear, where would be the sense of smell"* (1 Corinthians 12:14, 17)? In other words, some rock babies, some sing worship songs, some disciple students, some pray with intercession, some organize restoration projects in the community, some preach/teach Scripture, some greet guests, some clean toilets, some write encouraging notes, some lead trips to India, some track the budget on a spreadsheet, some plant flowers and trim hedges...etc.

But *all* are vital when invested.

And to the degree that any are *not* invested, or do not feel "vital," the whole is severely compromised in how it reveals the King's glory to the broader community.

God has given us to one another to help each other discover our particular role. Instead of creating a church culture that promotes some "parts" while overlooking others, a healthy, growing, living organism celebrates the individual contributions—no matter how small. Have you begun to embrace your place in the greatest living organism on the planet? It is always a good time to repent of our independence and renew our membership in the Body of Christ. Are you discovering and playing your particular role in its health and Kingdom impact? Imagine if every disciple of Jesus did!

STEWARDSHIP

My wife and I spent the summer of 1999 back in our hometown of Cincinnati, so that I could complete a pastoral internship as part of my graduate program. In order to maintain our place in married student housing, we arranged to rent our apartment to three college students while we were gone. It was a bit unnerving because we essentially entrusted all of our belongings to the safe keeping of relative strangers. We did the proper interviews and had the necessary paperwork filled out that ensured the retention of the deposit fee if anything were to get damaged. No particular piece had much value so we thought the deposit would do. Our new "tenants" seemed responsible enough, so we vacated in May with little concern.

Apparently, *too* **little.**

We arrived in August to a bit of a disaster. Before departing, we had explained with great clarity that, since the apartment was below ground, the one critical request was that they run the dehumidifier constantly throughout the summer; emptying the reservoir at least once a day. I specifically showed them where we keep it and how to run it, and they agreed to follow through. Much to our chagrin, however, they didn't. In fact, they didn't even run it once. So, we walked into our apartment to find multi-colored fuzzy mold growing in every nook and cranny. In the kitchen, for example, there was a circle of fuzz on the floor—a foot in diameter and a height of a couple of inches—a round mound of yellow and green mossy mold. We were beside ourselves.

In the ensuing weeks, we emptied our entire apartment of all its contents so that a restoration company could make it habitable again. In the process, we were forced to throw out most of our belongings, which were beyond recovery. When you're a poor grad student *that* is a major setback. We kept the deposit check, but when I pursued the negligent dwellers, they swore I had never mentioned the dehumidifier. In fact, from their perspective we owed *them* because one of them *"had the worst summer of her life"* trying to survive the moldy environment. I could hardly muster up any genuine compassion in the moment.

Two of the three were graduating and the third transferred. So the point was moot. Graciously, the Seminary helped us shoulder the cost of the recovery. Here's the life lesson: *don't trust college students*. (Ha! Just kidding.) Actually, the life lesson for us was

a good, *faithful* steward is worth
his/her weight in gold.

It's easy for me to condemn the students for their lack of care, careless oversight and misuse of our stuff. When I'm tempted to, however, I'm convicted within that I am equally guilty of the same crime when it comes to God's "stuff," which I am called to steward.

This is a revolutionary thought with which every disciple of King Jesus must come to terms. Scripture is consistent in its claim that everything in all the world ultimately belongs to God. In 1 Chronicles 29:11 King David prays, *"Yours, O Lord, is the greatness and the power and the glory and the victory and the majesty, for ALL that is in the heavens and in the earth is yours."* God Himself confirms this to Job: *"Who has first given to Me, that I should repay him? Whatever is under the whole heaven is Mine"* (Job 41:11). He doesn't say this with an air of hubris; it's just the way it is. And King David humbly concedes in Psalm 24:1 (quoted by Paul in 1 Corinthians 10:26): *"The earth is the Lord's and the fullness thereof."* Therefore, while by

American law we are "owners" of our own property—permitted to dispense with it as we please—our higher vocation has us serving as temporary managers of God's belongings. Think of your resources: opportunities, education, employment, property, relationships, health, energy, skills, interests...etc. When we yield to King Jesus, what we have is no longer ours by right. It is are ours by grace. It is all on loan to us to steward well for God's purposes. As disciples of Jesus

we are richly *entrusted* **in order that**
we might be faithfully *invested.*

Interestingly, the etymology of "steward" in Old English means "warden of the house." This parallels the New Testament Greek word for "steward": *oikonomos*. *Oikos* means "house" or "home," while *nomos* means "law" or "rule." So, "ruler or overseer of the home." We actually get our English word "economy" from *oikonomos*. It is the managed arrangement of the assets and financial opportunity of a given community. On an individual level we are each managers of particular assets that God has given to us both for our own joyful provision and for His Kingdom purposes.

It is the latter concept that's so *radical.*

It takes growth and maturity to willingly embrace the idea that a significant portion of what we've been given is actually intended for some*one* or some*thing* else. It's sort of like the mailmen that faithfully swing by every day: If they were to view themselves as the owner of the packages, they would sit under a tree in a park and have Christmas six days a week. As it is, they are stewards, not owners, entrusted with our mail for a time, not for their own consumption. Their vocation has them serving as couriers for our benefit and blessing (except the bills of course!). They own nothing in their little "British" cab (steering wheel on the right); they simply deliver as directed. This is to become our posture as well.

We are *couriers* **too.**

If we embrace our Christian vocation of stewardship, we will gladly deliver God's gifts to others. As Peter exhorts the Church: *"As each has received a gift, use it to serve one another, as good stewards of God's varied grace...in order that in everything God may be glorified through Jesus Christ"* (1 Peter 4:10-11). Literally, everything we are and have—talents, treasure, time—belong to God. We are called to give faithful oversight to His things, which means we are to be wise, faithful, even risk-taking investors in Kingdom ventures.

In Matthew 25:14-30, Jesus surprises us with a parable. (His parables were always surprising.) An owner of an estate, knowing he would be gone for a while, entrusts particular assets with three different stewards. In today's dollars it would equal about two million dollars total. While each steward is entrusted with a different amount, all three are charged to faithfully *invest* during his absence. Only two follow through. They double the value of the owner's resources, while the third squanders the opportunity by simply burying the treasure and doing nothing. The trustworthy stewards are honored and rewarded with greater oversight. The fearful, and perhaps lazy, fool is stripped of his role altogether. And the discipleship adage was born: *"For to everyone who has will more be given, and he will have an abundance"* (Matthew 25:29). That is, abundant personal provision to enjoy, but, more importantly, more of the King's assets to faithfully distribute as the King directs. *This* is what we're made for: not mere consumption of what we earn and own, but enjoyment and investment of what God has provided.

**Have you made this critical,
life-changing** *shift***?**

Most of us are content to elect Jesus "Mayor" of the religious town in our world, but He is only content reigning over the whole thing! Are you taking care of the physical body you've been given? It's God's gift to you. Are you allotting ample time in your schedule to pursue the things that matter most to Jesus, even trading "good" things for "best" things? Are you discovering how you are uniquely gifted by God, and are those gifts, passions, and interests finding expression in your local church—the living organism of which you are a part? Are you financially invested in the spiritual growth and Kingdom mission of your local church? The difference between a faithful steward and an ex-steward comes down to how we view all that we have at our disposal. What are we choosing to do with what God has provided us? How might the King be leading you to invest His resources?

GENEROSITY

A Sunday school teacher was finishing up a lesson on giving and asked, *"You know where little boys go if they don't put their money in the offering plate?"* A witty but ornery boy blurted out, *"Yes ma'am. They go to the movies!"* And we laugh. Because this *is* the reality, right? You either *give* your resources away, or you *spend* them. You may also save them, but that is just delayed spending or eventual giving.

Money is the *currency* of life.

That's why we're always trying to make more of it, multiply it, protect it, and stretch it as far as it can go. Because every single day, life is dramatically affected by money. It's a pretty big deal. So it is fitting for us to do a bit of a spiritual gut-check on the role money plays in our lives as disciples of Jesus. If *all* of life matters to King Jesus, then He isn't content with a mere slice. He wants it ALL! And that includes our money. Jesus literally spent a fifth of his teaching career coaching His disciples on "dough." Not because He thought it was intrinsically bad, but because He knew it wasn't automatically good. If King Jesus is in His rightful place, money can be a great personal blessing and a great kingdom asset. If, however, money's enthroned, then it hinders God's work in our lives and in His world.

Jesus says, *"For where your treasure is, there your heart will be also. No one can serve two masters, for either he will hate the one and love the other, or he will be devoted to the one and despise the other. You cannot serve God and money"* (Matthew 6:21, 24). Did He know this would be an issue for us or what? What do you look to for what matters most: your identity, your security, your provision, your significance? For most of us it has something to do with the mighty dollar. So, life's goal often becomes making as much of it as we can. At times, even sacrificing physical and emotional health and even meaningful relationships to make more. Sometimes even cutting corners and sacrificing ethics to get there.

We see it all the time. And it's not just "them out there"; it's a wrestling within each of us. Every rung on the ladder has a certain dollar amount connected to it. We're all too easily enticed to stretch for that next rung. We're lured by the prospect of getting just a little more.

When what matters most *depends* on money, guess what gets enthroned?

Money charts the course. It sets the calendar of our lives and decides *what* we can do and even *who* we can become. In this sense, it is god-like. And that's Jesus' point. There can only be one God.

"Giving" is natural to God. He is always invested in others. It's His reflex. "Consuming" is natural to us. Yet, when God calls you and you choose to follow Jesus, His Spirit gets busy within you, remaking you into *His* image, turning insatiable consumers into generous Kingdom-investors like Him. And this is an act of love, because God the Father wants to preserve us from an unhealthy relationship with currency. If I know a bridge across a creek won't hold my daughter, isn't it love if I point it out? God knows that

money can't bear the *weight* of our longings.

He also knows that one of the greatest keys to developing a healthy relationship with money is beginning to practice the art of giving. Intentional generosity actually sets you free from the prison of unquenchable acquisition and consumption.

For the apostle Paul, one of the greatest illustrations of this is found in the generous spirit of Jesus' disciples in Macedonia. The Corinthians gladly responded to the gospel, but the influence of the surrounding pagan culture was getting the best of them. So as an antidote, Paul promotes generous giving. We find three critical components in 2 Corinthians 8—faith, worship, and joy.

First, generous giving is an act of faith. *"In a severe test of affliction, their abundance of joy and their extreme poverty have overflowed in a wealth of generosity"* (2 Corinthians 8:2). Economic times were not good. Their circumstances did not promote generous giving, but their faith in a generous God did. The contrast

213

is striking. Corinth had vast wealth, but was *impoverished* in faith and giving. We're not told how much these eager investors gave, but it was generous, and even sacrificial: *"For they gave according to their means...and beyond their means, of their own accord"* (2 Corinthians 8:3).

They were compelled from *within*!

This is one of the reasons why I personally don't promote a specific percentage. Some scholars and Christians set the amount at 10%, carrying over the Temple tax from the Old Testament—the "tithe" ("a tenth") that God required of Israel to care for the Temple and its civil proceedings. While I am a bit suspect of applying the Temple tax from Israel's theocracy directly to the Church, it's hard for me to imagine that after receiving Gospel grace—the gift of the Cross and the Holy Spirit—our generosity would fall *below* theirs. Many disciples justify giving little on the basis that the "tithe" is nowhere required in the New Testament. Perhaps its silence, however, is due to the fact that God anticipates more, not less. After all, in Luke 21:1-4 Jesus honors the widow because she gave everything she had. We naturally want it to be about the box that *we* check, and God always makes it about our hearts that *He* checks.

So how do you know how much to invest in the Church? Well, we have to start engaging God directly on the matter. After all, if we're *His* stewards, we need to get direction from *Him*. This is what these Greek Christians did. Paul reports, *"...they gave themselves first to the Lord and then by the will of God to us"* (2 Corinthians 8:5). That's a healthy rhythm.

Their investment was the *overflow* of worship.

They invited God to have His way in them and He led them to invest in the Church. Instead of squeezing Jesus into a quadrant of life, they were seeking to yield all of it to Him. So, they were free to release *His* resources for *His* purposes as He saw fit.

Is that becoming true of you? Are you willing to begin praying regularly a version of this prayer:

> *Thank you Father for all your many provisions.*
> *What portion of what you've given to me*
> *do you intend to give through me?*

Sometimes God will lead you to *enjoy* His provision. Give Him thanks for every tangible morsel. Sometimes, however, as an act of faith and worship, He'll ask you to invest, actually invite you to participate in *His* work in *His* Church. Believe it or not, generous giving can actually become a privilege. It certainly was for our Macedonian siblings. Paul tells us they were "*...begging us earnestly for the favor of taking part in the relief of the saints*" (2 Corinthians 8:4).

As long as investing in the Church feels like a personal loss or a disappointing extraction, there's still a fair amount of heart work that needs to be done between us and Jesus. He wants to get us to the point where it's one of our greatest joys! What is Jesus saying to your heart right now? Is there gratitude? Conviction? Are you asking him for His perspective on your investment of His resources? Is your generosity reflective of God's provision? Are you giving in *faith*, where you will have to trust God to come through? Are you giving as *worship*, inviting Him to lead you? And is giving becoming a *joy*? Let's probe that radical thought a bit more together.

PLEASURE

While the crazed hustle of December annually leads me to the emotional ledge, I can say with complete sincerity that Christmas morning is one of my favorite times of the year. Of course this was true in my childhood because I would receive gifts I had dreamed of getting for months. Now, however, as an adult, and as a parent in particular, it is a great day because of the joy I find in watching anticipation give birth to glad satisfaction. Kids are always amazed that we parents know just what they *"always wanted."*

Gift receiving is so fun. But actually, the anticipation-to-satisfaction process to which I refer is the joy each of my children takes in giving gifts to one another. *That* is the best!

**The *giver* anticipates
the joy of the *recipient*.**

At least for one morning a jealousy truce is upheld in our home as each child finds great pleasure in watching a sibling open a gift from *them*. Now, the youngest ones don't have a dime to their name (unless they recently lost a tooth!), so the gift they give is paid in full by "yours truly." We gladly enrich our kids to *enable* their generosity. And their enthusiasm blows us away. It's convicting actually. When we give them money to shop, the thought never occurs to them to spend it on themselves. With joy they dream up their idea, with joy they travel to the store, with joy they hunt down just the right gift, and with joy they wrap it and give it. They're actually grateful to us for helping them have something to give.

**And *that* is the height of
biblical stewardship and generosity.**

Think for a moment about the ground we've covered. In our first theme we pivoted from the myth of *independence* to the truth of *inter-dependence*, embracing our significant place as a member of a larger, living organism. Then we challenged the deep-seated myth of *ownership* and instead embraced the truth of *stewardship*, where everything we are and have belongs to God. Furthermore, we tackled the mythical virtue of *miserliness*, recognizing that we are called instead to lavish *generosity* as an act of faith and worship. And now finally, there's a theme of pleasure. Here's a fourth myth: *"I may have to give, but I don't have to like it!"* This reminds me of the obstinate child who, after having resisted obedience for a great long while, finally sat down on the chair. Though seated, his stubborn will persisted as his grumpy face spoke with clarity: *"I may be sitting down, but I'm standing up on the inside."* Well, when it comes to the Christian life,

> *how* **we do** *what* **we do is as important,**
> **as our doing** *anything* **at all.**

It's a humbling admission, but God doesn't need our resources to accomplish His purposes. However, He has wisely and graciously chosen to enrich us so that we might have something to give. As our loving Father, God knows the joy of giving lavishly—even giving His own Son for our redemption—so He gladly equips us with resources (time, talent, treasure) so that we can enter into His joy! As long as giving generously is an obligatory extraction (like getting your wisdom teeth pulled!) you will struggle to find joy in investing in the Church. But if, by the Holy Spirit, reluctant foot-dragging is transformed into cheerful investment of God's resources, with which He has graciously endowed us, who knows what soul satisfaction could awaken within. Ironically, mature

217

generosity looks an awful lot like child-like gift-giving. It is to become our pleasure to invest in what God is doing among and through His people.

After teaching the Corinthian Christians about generosity in 2 Corinthians 8, Paul turns to this deeper objective of finding pleasure in investing. He challenges them to be ready to give *"as a willing gift, not as an exaction"* (2 Corinthians 9:5) and *"to sow bountifully instead of sparingly"* promising that they *"will also reap bountifully"* (2 Corinthians 9:6). This is perhaps a lost motivation for us. While Paul is vague about the particular nuance of the promised "bounty," he's quite clear that a blessing of some sort is due the joyfully generous investor. Of course this is not a "Get Rich!" scheme—sowing money in order to get more. It *is*, however, a joyful giving strategy where we take great delight in the giving because we're confident the Kingdom return will be worth it.

Again, the core issue is the *posture* of our heart.

Paul clarifies in 2 Corinthians 9:7, *"Each one must give as he has decided in his heart, not reluctantly or under compulsion, for God loves a cheerful giver."* While we do not go in and out of the redemptive love of God on the basis of how much or how joyfully we give, the Father's delight in us certainly grows as His generous heart comes alive in us. As a parent, I can certainly testify to that. I love all of my children equally (at least I seek to), but I take greater pleasure in their generous moments than I do when they choose to be stingy with their resources (or mine!). This is reminiscent of the joy King David took in his people as he witnessed their lavish, joyful investments in the Temple. *"The people rejoiced because they had given willingly, for with a whole heart they had offered freely to the Lord. David the King also rejoiced greatly"* (1 Chronicles 29:9). Or, *"...now I have seen your people...offering freely and joyously to you"* (1 Chronicles 29:17). A vibrant sign of spiritual maturity is the awakening of an inner pleasure as you invest in the Church.

And just to reiterate, this joyful investment is made possible by God Himself.

He invests *in* us
so that He can invest *through* us.

King David acknowledges this: *"Who are we that we should be able thus to offer willingly? For all things come from you, and of your own have we given you. O Lord our God, all this abundance that we have provided...comes from your hand and is all your own"* (1 Chronicles 29:14, 16). Joyful generosity is possible because God endows us with resources to invest. Paul confirms this in 2 Corinthians 9:8 *"God is able to make all grace abound to you, so that having all sufficiency in all things at all times, you may abound in every good work."* Even promising, *"you will be enriched in every way to be generous in every way"* (2 Corinthians 9:11).

This is true, by the way, of *all* the resources
God entrusts to us.

Financial giving is just one aspect, but serving the local church with our investment of time, energy, skills, and passions is of equal importance. And here again, by the Holy Spirit, God equips us to make a meaningful contribution to the Church. In Romans 12:6 Paul says, we have *"gifts that differ according to the grace given to us."* Or again, *"there are a variety of activities, but it is the same God who empowers them all in everyone. To each is given the manifestation of the Spirit for the common good. And these are empowered by one and the same*

Spirit, who apportions to each one individually as He wills" (1 Corinthians 12:4-7, 11).

So, why do you think we talk ourselves out of either making a significant contribution or doing so with great joy? It's grace from start to finish. God welcomes us by grace, changes us by grace, and even equips us by grace. He does all this so that we might find great pleasure in playing our part in the growing maturity and Kingdom impact of our church. Are you catching this vision? Our grateful hearts ought to echo with tangible investment. What is one action step you can take in the coming weeks to affirm your glad commitment to your local church? Remember, by grace you are

a *part* **of something** *bigger*!

"Thank You for graciously restoring the broken pieces of my life.

Please give me Your compassionate heart today to identify real need around me,

and the courage to play my part in restoring brokenness across the street and around the world."

9

RESTORE

the Broken

Gratitude – Compassion – Courage – Wholeness

INTRODUCTION

I was painting my daughter's room and came across a crack in the seam near the ceiling. Initially I thought I could paint over it, believing it was superficial. Nothing like a fresh coat of paint to cover the cracks. I tested it with my finger, however, and realized that it was far more significant than I'd imagined. The more I probed, the more obvious the gap appeared.

It didn't need to be covered;
it needed *repair.*

So the cutting and the spackling commenced, and the broken wall was eventually restored.

As I was fixing it, I was reminded of a similar situation with the daughter whose room I was painting. Every parent approaches the birth of a child hoping and praying that everything will go smoothly—mom sustained, labor swift, baby healthy. The birth of our fourth went according to this plan. She was an adorable little bundle and we were grateful. Which was appropriate since it was just two weeks before Thanksgiving. Perfect timing to travel to relatives for the holiday and share our new addition. Of course, they all loved her.

The Norman Rockwell moment, however, didn't last the weekend. In the middle of the night, our little girl was unusually warm. Like the minor crack in the wall, I shrugged it off initially, attributing it to that little newborn skullcap the hospital provides. The more I touched her forehead, however, the more I realized it was fever-hot and she was way too young for a fever. She was broken and needed repair.

So, we made the 2 a.m. trip to Children's Hospital in Cincinnati. The doctors and nurses were great, but they couldn't initially diagnose her malady. Their fear was meningitis, so they chose to do a spinal tap. It was the right course, but an exceedingly painful procedure. I'd never felt so helpless and her wail only magnified my feelings of inadequacy. Unlike the crack in her eventual bedroom wall, she was broken and I didn't know how to fix her.

Thankfully, the medical community did. Eventually, they discovered a rare abnormality and gently nursed her back to health. We thanked them profusely as healing came, and with a gracious, compassionate smile they'd often say, *"That's what we're here for."* And it wasn't prideful, it was just honest. This is what they wanted to do; this is what they trained to do.

They *aim* to restore the broken.

The longer I walk with Jesus, the more I realize that restoring brokenness is a significant part of what *we're* here for as His disciples. When you open the Gospels and meet Jesus for the first time, over and over you find Him seeking out the broken, the marginalized, the hurting and hiding, the overlooked. Jesus had eyes for and was tenderhearted toward those who probably gave up hope of healing long ago. Physical ailments, emotional wounds, spiritual doubts...Jesus saw it all. And rather than just moving on with His own agenda—*painting the crack*—time and again Jesus slows down long enough to engage the broken at the point of their need, and tend to the shattered pieces of their lives.

What we might naturally see as inconvenient interruptions, Jesus saw as Gospel-grace opportunities. The brokenness around Him wasn't in the way of His ministry, it *was* His ministry. Broken people are why He came! As He would eventually explain to the "religious" in Matthew 9:12-13, who acted like they had it all together, *"Those who are well have no need of a physician, but those who are sick. I desire mercy not sacrifice. I came not to call the righteous, but sinners."*

Why do we spend so much energy painting over the *cracks* in our lives?

Somehow, we convince ourselves that covering them up makes them go away. But it never does. We can don the façade all we want, but underneath we are all busted and broken. And for so many reasons. While New Creation is breaking in and its fullness is on the way, we *do* live in a still fallen world. Sticks and stones aside, we're vulnerable to the shattering words and choices of others. We're broken because we've broken ourselves and because we're opposed by an enemy that wants to undermine our wholeness. When you put all of that together, you understand why we have fallen into so many pieces.

Yet most of us remain rigorously committed to putting on a show, as if everything's just fine. We don't want anyone to see us sweat, so we often choose to cope anonymously, in hiding. We often fail to realize that

the path to *healing* **begins**
where the *hiding* **ends.**

We get so familiar with the aches and pains of life, we can't imagine life without them. And our pride imprisons us. Why are we so reticent to admit our need for restoration, especially when the need is universal in everyone we meet?

Look in on Jesus again. What do you see Him doing? Who do you see Him engaging? He eagerly feeds the hungry, courageously touches and heals the leper, surprisingly defends the prostitute, and graciously confronts the adulterer. He gives sight to the blind and the gift of forgiveness to the unsuspecting sinner. He humbles the high and mighty, folds in the outcast, and lifts up the downcast. Why does Jesus dine with the 'scoundrels'?

Because He *loves* **them.**

And because He wants to convince us all that if we're willing to ask, He's willing to restore *our* brokenness too.

Are there *pieces* in your life that need repair? Where are you less than whole? Where are you not "enough"? The only prerequisite for healing is finally admitting you can't fix yourself. That's when

Jesus begins to do His greatest work. Which readies you for a big surprise! As Jesus restores you, something else begins to happen inside. As restoration arrives, you discover a growing desire to participate in the restoration of others. Jesus turns us inside out, giving us an outward, missional focus to see others as He sees them. Now, by His Spirit,

King Jesus restores others *through* **the restored.**

Just like with the lifelong priority of PURSUE—where the pursued become pursuers, so also the restored become restorers. Pursuing future disciples and restoring the broken are simply two sides of the same Missional coin. In PURSUE, we cultivate relationships with those outside the faith as the entry point of Gospel grace, whereas, in RESTORE, Gospel grace arrives with our awareness and availability to tend to the real needs of those around us.

Every single day there's tangible brokenness all around us. Whether it's people we work with or live near, the lady at the grocery store, the mechanic doing our oil change, the orphan in Uganda who needs sponsoring, or the lonely woman in the pew who just needs to be noticed, God deliberately places broken people in our paths and invites us to be a part of their restoration. They are not inconvenient interruptions, they are Gospel opportunities. Does your heart break over the brokenness of others? Are you willing to be a part of their wholeness? The Restorer Himself is willing to grow us there. Let's learn this together.

GRATITUDE

It was the summer of 1999 and my wife and I had only two children (we would eventually have seven)—a two-year-old son and a four-month-old daughter. We packed our rickety old blue Mercedes Benz wagon to the gills for our 900-mile journey from Boston to Cincinnati. Unfortunately, about 300 miles into the trip, the wagon began to sputter with billows of smoke wafting out the rear of the car, followed by an awful groaning noise. The car began losing power so I began looking for a safe place to pull off. Thankfully, an exit was just an eighth of a mile ahead: *Utica, NY.*

The car limped off the ramp, lurching and stopping over and over, as though we were riding an untamed, temperamental donkey. We quickly discovered there was a Master Mercedes mechanic in town, and, though it was near the end of the day on Friday, he was pleased to take us in. What a gracious, generous man. God provided a Christian brother when we needed one most. We actually fellowshipped together in his office while his mechanics nursed our car back to health. Here we were in a back alley of Utica, NY, certainly a bit put out by the disruption, but totally set at ease because of this kind mechanic.

Fast forward three months.

Having spent the summer in Cincinnati, it was time to return to Boston. In route, our rickety old car began making a terrible grinding noise, which just got louder and louder. Admittedly, I was frustrated as we limped off the exit ramp, wondering, *"What am I going to do with my little family at midnight in the middle of nowhere?"* After checking three of the local hotels and finding no vacancies (does this sound biblical?), we were forced to go to the "A-1 Motel." I've never seen a greater dive. The man at the desk had good news and bad news. The good news was they *did* have one room left. The bad news was...they *did* have one room left. And we *had* to take it. I told my wife that it would be best if she just climbed into bed without turning on the lights. It was *that* bad. Yet waking up the next morning, not having at least experienced any roaches or spiders, I found myself thankful for the A-1. After securing breakfast from a vending machine, I opened the yellow pages to look for a mechanic. To my shock, we were in Utica, NY all over again!

What are the chances of breaking down at the same exit twice on a 900-mile trip with a three-month span in between? My wife remembered the mechanic's name, I called him up, and after we had a good chuckle, he took our car in. He restored it *again* and sent us back on our way. Our hearts were filled with thanksgiving to God for His tangible, gracious provision. Utica, NY, will always represent God's glad desire to *restore* us. Might that old Benz serve as a picture of each of our lives in desperate need of restoration? We come into this world in pieces because of our union with broken humanity, which is only exacerbated by our own sinful choices and the choices of others that break us even more. We all try to "hold it together,"

but *broken* is our common experience.

We're all in need of repair, to be made more whole than ever before. And this is why Jesus came.

The Gospel accounts—Matthew, Mark, Luke, and John— catalogue Jesus' compassionate courage to restore broken people. And the proper response to being restored is *gratitude*! Gratitude is the posture a heart takes when one's real need and sense of unworthiness is met by a surprisingly delightful provision.

What can you do but be *glad*?

And our gratitude is welcomed by our Restorer.

We see this play out in Luke 17:11-19 where Jesus graciously restores ten lepers. The ten cry out to Jesus for mercy and Jesus delights to show mercy, sending them on their way and healing them as they go. For them, it's like a resurrection as they receive their lives back: their bodies, their families, their vocations, and their place in society.

Imagine their joy.

And yet, surprisingly, we're given no sense that gratitude was the prevailing response. In fact, only one returns to Jesus: *"...when he saw that he was healed, he turned back, praising God with a loud voice; and he fell on his face at Jesus' feet, giving him thanks"* (Luke 17:15-16). This is an amazing moment in the Gospel because the restored man is "praising God" while he is falling at the feet of Jesus. In other words, those who are restored glorify God by honoring Christ. And notice, Jesus does not rebuke him for blasphemy, but instead receives his gratitude as completely appropriate. Since King Jesus is God in person—Restorer of the broken, He alone is worthy of our gratitude. It's an incredible scene.

We see something similar with the woman at the well in John 4. Interestingly, another Samaritan. Jesus deliberately sought out Samaritans because they were the ultimate outcasts in Israel, viewed by most Jews as half-bred sell-outs who had given up their pure Jewish blood for a tainted, pagan, Gentile mix. Jesus knew that, if He was to convince those watching that His restoration was genuine and even intended for the whole world, He would have to confront some of the most deeply rooted prejudices and taboos. Greeting a woman, a woman He does not know, a Samaritan, in broad daylight was about as risky as it could get. Yet Jesus saw her as worth the risk.

He *always* **does.**

Jesus initiates a conversation with her about "thirst" as a metaphorical way of unearthing her heartache. He offers her a drink that will satisfy her forever in contrast to the well, to which she must return over and over. Initially, she welcomes the offer of this "miracle" water, only to discover that Jesus is actually dialing in on her personal brokenness, which goes far deeper than temporary, physical thirst. He invites her to fetch her husband, to which she replies, *"I have no husband"*(John 4:17). On its face this is true, but in reality, she has been going in and out of marital relationships for years, trying to slake her "thirst" in the arms of one man after another. Jesus knows this and wants to restore her and make her new. Armed with nothing but compassion and courage, He shatters societal custom and fully reveals Himself to her: *"I who speak to you am He (the Messiah)"* (John 4:26).

And she was *changed.*

Leaving her jar at the well, with gratitude fueling her sprint, she ran to tell the whole town who she had found. Or perhaps more accurately, who had found her! And we learn, *"Many Samaritans from the town believed in Him because of the woman's testimony....and many more believed...*saying, *'...this is indeed the Savior of the world'"* (John 4:39, 41-42). Her joyful restoration led to the restoration of others. And *that* is by design.

How about you? What specific form has brokenness taken in your life? How has He mended you? Does your heart well up with gratitude to God for the restorative work He *has* and *is* doing in you? Gratitude is to become our growing lifestyle. As Paul says in 1 Thessalonians 5:16-18, *"Rejoice always, pray without ceasing, and give thanks in all circumstances; for this is the will of God in Christ Jesus for you.*" Every circumstance is not pleasing to be sure, but there is reason for thanksgiving even in the midst of the hardest of times. Because God is at work. Is your growing vertical gratitude spilling over the rim of your life horizontally as you testify to your gospel restoration? What keeps us from going there? Why do we often withhold the best news ever?

COMPASSION

My favorite pop album growing up was unquestionably *Joshua Tree* by the timeless rock band U2. So many great singles from one record. As it turns out, totally by coincidence, I actually have a *Joshua Tree* in my back yard. At least that's what we call it. It is a Maple and it used to reside in the middle of the woods behind our home. One fall day, my then 11-year-old son and I were attempting to free about ten trees in the forest from suffocating vines. These massive, vertical gnarly roots were choking the life out of these innocent trees. So with saws and hatchets and axes in hand we set out to deliver them from certain demise and restoring them to their original beauty.

In the process, we stumbled along a little sapling that was only about two-feet tall. Buried under the thick canopy of taller trees, it had minimal access to the sun and no chance of surviving, let alone thriving. My son said, "Dad, shouldn't we dig this one up and move it out into the sun?" Perhaps because I was too focused on the vine-task at hand, or because I was naturally suspicious of any agricultural insight coming from a Kirk, let alone a young one, I initially dismissed the idea as untenable. When we finished our job, however, he persisted. I *conceded* on the grounds that there was nothing really to lose. He proceeded on the grounds that there was a tree to be gained. He saw *potential* in this fledgling maple and was willing to put in the time to gently transplant it from a broken environment into one where it might flourish. While the odds seemed stacked against this outcome, over seven years later I can humbly and actually with great joy admit that our Joshua Tree is now twelve-feet tall and spreading new branches and leaves every year.

The reality is, if we have eyes to see and hearts prepared to respond

there are Joshua Trees *all around* **us.**

There are men, women, and children who are currently being overlooked, whom society has cast aside, whose restoration and ultimate flourishing appears on its face to be "untenable," but who have great potential. The contributing factors are too numerous to number: multiple broken marriages, chaotic family systems, early exposure to misguided behavior, sexual wounds, chemical dependencies, jaded bitterness, laziness, entitlement, pent-up anger, layers of deceit, broken promises...etc. Whatever the root cause, however, *broken* is how many begin every day.

And *hopelessness* **is the eventual fruit**
of stringing too many broken days together.

Profitable change seems so implausible.

Heartbreak morphs into heartache, which often gives birth to callous and numb affections. No longer capable of caring for themselves, the broken can become reluctant to be cared for at all. While their plight is terribly unfortunate, it's familiar to them and so the prospect of being delivered almost becomes undesirable.

Thriving becomes even more impossible than a pipe-dream, and even simply surviving hardly seems feasible.

The broken often need someone else to believe for them, to see the potential glory that resides within them as bearers of God's imprinted image.

And that's where multiplying disciples come in.

Out of grateful obedience, we take our cues from King Jesus Himself, who not only calls us to play our part in restoring the broken among us, but models for us what a compelling heart of compassion looks like. There's a curious Greek word— *splanchnizomai*—that appears multiple times in the four Gospel accounts. Etymologically, the word refers to the movement of one's inner organs (e.g. the heart, liver, intestines...etc.). It is a dramatic word that takes compassion to a whole new level. It was not sufficient for Jesus to simply "feel sorry" for the broken around Him, offering only a half-hearted, temporary patronization; rather Jesus was physically moved, internally compelled to meet their tangible needs. We find the remnants of this intensely vivid meaning in our English expressions: "a visceral reaction" or "gut-wrenching." This is not an emotion that leaves one wishing things were different; it is an internal conviction that they *must* be different, and a commitment to seeing the difference come to fruition. It is the inability to move forward without making an attempt at participating in restoration.

This **is Jesus**

And we see it time and time again. The same Jesus that challenges His disciples in Matthew 25 to feed the hungry, slake the thirsty, welcome the stranger, clothe the naked, and visit the sick and imprisoned modeled it many times before. In Mark 1:41 Jesus is *"moved with pity,"* willingly touching a leper no one would touch in order to heal him. "Pity" is a paltry translation as this is the visceral, gut-wrenching compassion of God in person. Things aren't as they should be,

**and King Jesus has come
to make them** *new.*

Likewise, in Luke 7 Jesus' heart throbs for a widow who is burying her only son. He comforts her saying, *"Do not weep"* (Luke 7:13) and then raises her son and restores him to her. Or, in Matthew 9:36, we're told that, when Jesus saw the crowds full of broken people, he had deep compassion, longing to shepherd the *"harassed and helpless."* And in Matthew 20:31, we find the crowd attempting to silence two blind men, calling out to Jesus. Jesus shocks the crowd by gladly interrupting His planned journey from Jericho to Jerusalem in order to personally touch their eyes and restore their sight. They weren't in the way of His mission; they *were* His mission. Matthew roots this surprising mercy in Jesus' visceral compassion for broken people. He had every intention of redeeming the souls of those around Him, but He gladly saw their tangible infirmity as part of His mission too.

As His disciples, we're to walk in His footsteps. *"If anyone has the world's goods and sees his brother in need, yet closes his heart against him, how does God's love abide in him"* (1 John 3:17)? In other words,

if God's deep compassion *for* **you
is finding its home** *in* **you,
it will make its way** *out.*

And as it does, Jesus explains in Matthew 25:40 this sobering and thrilling reality: *"As you did it to one of the least of these my brothers, you did it to me."* Jesus is so passionate for the broken that He identifies with them personally, completely. Their plight is His plight. Therefore, our tangible compassion for the broken literally loves on Jesus in a special way. This is uniquely true within the Body of Christ—with our Christian siblings, but time and again Jesus' ministry models that this compassion has no bounds. No one is outside His restorative reach.

What a *radical* **life!**

God calls us to learn to love like Jesus. Think right now of those whom God has placed specifically around you. Who is in your reach, a "Joshua Tree" just waiting to be noticed, tended to, and restored? Might you begin to pray that God would move you deeply—in the bowels of your soul—over the brokenness of others? And as *His* heart becomes yours, pray that He might give you the courage to play your part. You are likely not the sole solution and it is not your burden to carry their entire load. So, you'll have to discern with wisdom whether or not the Spirit is prompting you to participate. But don't too quickly jettison the thought and abandon the broken. Engaging them is risky. But if Jesus is in it, the greater risk is to walk away and do nothing. We need Jesus' courage to grow in us alongside His compassion. It is to this bold and carefree courage that we turn next.

COURAGE

Picture a stranded family along the interstate in obvious distress. The mother sits on a tattered suitcase, hair uncombed, clothes in disarray. She has a glazed look to her eyes, and holds a smelly, poorly clothed, crying baby. The father is unshaven, in coveralls, despairing as he tries to corral two other youngsters. Beside them sits an old jalopy which has just breathed its last. Coincidentally, a man from the Red Cross comes barreling down the road. The father waves, but the man just drives on by. Soon another car comes. This one is driven by a Pastor late for church. He's moved to slow down, but decides there just isn't time, and drives on by. Thankfully, the third car stops. The driver is an outspoken atheist from the ACLU who has never been to church a day in his life. Yet, when he sees the broken family, he takes them into his own car. After inquiring as to their need, he takes them to a local motel, pays for a week's lodging while the father finds work, and gives the mother cash for food and new clothes.

Surprise!

We're all expecting an Evangelical Christian to stop and assist, so we're brought up short when an atheist plays the role of hero. The story's twist forces the revealing question: *"Would I have stopped?"*

Jesus' parables had this effect on religious people in the first century too. He caught people off guard by meeting them on *their* turf, engaging them within their cultural context, drawing them into a dialogue, and then springing the trap!

And we're *all* caught.

Jesus' parables disarm us and then cut our hearts with an unexpected twist. This artistry is perhaps on greatest display in Jesus' teaching about the "Good Samaritan" (Luke 10:25-37), where He answers the question: *"Who is my neighbor?"*

A teacher of the Law asks Jesus to clarify His call to love God wholeheartedly and to love one's neighbor as one loves oneself. At first blush it appears innocent enough: *"Who should I love, Jesus?"* But beneath the pure veneer is an implicit and more devious inquiry: *"Who am I free not to love?"* As a Jew with ingrained, generational prejudice against pagan sinners in particular, he fears Jesus is asking for the moon. Surely not.

But of course Jesus *is*.

Genuine love for God overflows with tangible love for others, especially those *nobody* loves. Jesus modeled this with the broken— the prostitutes, tax collectors, lepers, adulterers...etc., and He makes His point through a compelling story.

When I was in college I walked a portion of the treacherous Jericho Road and was nearly thrown off the narrow path as Bedouins came around a very tight curve. Camels are huge in real life and do not yield to oncoming traffic. Jesus describes a very real place. A Jew could easily have been beaten, robbed, and left unconscious and in Jesus' story one was. One would think the arrival of a Jewish priest would be good news. Yet, the priest rationalizes why it would be unwise to help, and moves along.

**How easily we *rationalize* away
our *responsibility* to restore the broken?**

A Levite—an associate priest—is the next to discover the man. He at least stops to examine him. Yet, like the priest before him, he chooses not to be inconvenienced by this anonymous victim. We always have our reasons to remain uninvolved, don't we? Brokenness is often very messy. Who has the time or the energy to come to the aid of the broken? Jesus' listeners are wondering how this story will resolve.

Not as they imagined, that's for sure.

Knowing they presume the "hero" to be a Jewish laymen like themselves, Jesus offers a most outrageous and insulting twist: the hero is a *Samaritan*. Jewish and Samaritan hatred dated back centuries. Jesus couldn't have chosen a more controversial figure as the restorer in His story.

Like the two before him, the Samaritan *sees* the man and certainly has reason to pass by—time, inconvenience, threat of danger. Unlike the Priest and the Levite, however, the Samaritan is *moved from within* by what he sees. Do you remember *splanchnizomai* from the previous section? Here it is again. This man's deepest core is wrenched for his presumed enemy. Can you imagine? His courage completes his compassion, as he jumps in to assist. He tenderly nurses the man's wounds by softening them with oil, disinfecting them with wine, and bandaging them up. Ironic, as oil and wine would have been two elements the Priest and the Levite would likely have had on them as they returned from serving in the Temple. Each had resources; only the Samaritan made his available.

Great courage, costly mercy.

He touches the victim, takes him in his arms, and gives him his colt to ride to safety. He pays the dues of the inn and then some, even promising to return to clear any debt incurred in his absence.

Now, remember, the teacher of the Law merely wanted to know: *"Who is my neighbor?"* Or better: *"Who is not my neighbor?"* Where are the boundaries of this call to radical love? Yet, Jesus presses him to consider the boundless love of God instead. Those who truly receive it will want to pass it on. Jesus closes with one final question: *"Which of these three proved to be a neighbor to the man who fell among the robbers"* (Luke 10:36)? The man correctly answers, *"The one who showed him mercy."* (Luke 10:37). Which is true, but incomplete. He's not quite able to identify the hero as a "Samaritan" is he? *"You go,"* Jesus says, *"and do likewise"* (Luke 10:37). Imitate this mercy. Courageously respond to the visceral compassion moving you from within. Cultivate a heart for the broken. Pray and prepare to play a part in their restoration.

The Father's gracious plan to reach the globe was not to have His Son Jesus reach everyone Himself, but to reach others through *us*, embodying Himself in all of our communities. Those who have experienced restorative grace become the restorers of the broken around them. *This* is God's plan. As God's love finds its home in you, you are changed from the inside out and can hardly contain the love. Brokenness around you makes you restless with a holy discontent, eager to be a part of the solution. This Samaritan-love can take so many different shapes.

Our paths are *strewn* with opportunities to meet real need.

It could take the form of tangible acts of kindness toward your direct neighbors—to your left and to your right, and across the street. Do you know their names? Are you intentionally getting to know their *lives*? It is difficult to know their hidden brokenness if we aren't getting to know them. Maybe there's a co-worker or a boss, a teacher or fellow student. Somebody at the fitness club, or the country club, or Kiwanis. Fellow parents at the PTA or out on the soccer fields. *Can you see them?* Not just people with faces, but precious lives with real needs, most of which are often hidden. Yet silently, behind the façade, marriages are falling apart, parenting isn't going well, and addictions of many kinds are stealing life from our neighbors. Do we care? Do I *really* care?

Consider those *without* resource, and not just the needy around you. Perhaps *"Ignorance is bliss!"* because knowledge is responsibility. Technology has made the *world* our community. We know so much. We simply know too much to press on naïvely, acting like we don't hear the cry. And while it is not our role to shoulder the entire load, it would be helpful and potentially life-changing if we each committed to shouldering part of it. I think it was Bono who said, *"Tear a little corner off the darkness."* As we rightly enjoy God's pleasing provisions, are we also discerning what entrusted provisions He intends for us to share with others? As glad recipients of His grace, we're to be channels of that grace as well. That's what we call PURSUE. As giddy recipients of His blessings, we're to be channels of them too. That's what we call RESTORE.

God often provides *for* His world
through His people.

What is one tangible way God might be calling you to participate in His restoration of a single life? There are so many possibilities. Might you sponsor a child? Might you learn about foster care? Have you ever considered adoption? Is there a single parent you could come alongside of to lighten their load? Have you ever thought about mentoring or tutoring elementary school children? Is there a family with a special needs child that could benefit from your offer of respite care? Might you volunteer a portion of your month stocking a food bank? The list of potential opportunities is endless.

What will it be for you?

At the very least, it's being more mindful today of the people around you and deliberately engaging them. Your next waiter or waitress. The woman at the check-out or the teller at the bank. The next call-out at your church to join in a restore project. Take a risk and jump in!

Why do our fears hinder us from helping? Have you received the Samaritan love of Jesus? Become the Samaritan to somebody and join Jesus in His work in His world. He's the restorer, but He's chosen to include us in His mission. What a meaningful gift!

WHOLENESS

I woke up around midnight. It was the dead of winter. I had fallen asleep on the couch under a warm blanket watching a sporting event. I slowly stumbled up to bed. Reaching the top I was reminded by an overflowing trashcan that it was *garbage night*. "Ugh!" In my house it's like a three-hour project (slight exaggeration). Did I mention that it was cold and I was really tired? Everyone but me was fast asleep, cozy in their beds. I grumbled a little as I dragged those cans to the curb through a foot of snow. Alright, the snow part was added for effect. I did grumble though. But I got all the garbage out.

When I began to ascend the stairs again, I noticed one light was still on. So I went back down, turned off the bathroom light, only to discover the toilet needed flushing. Am I the only dad who thinks "flushing drills" should be mandatory training in our schools? I

RESTORE the Broken

flushed the toilet, walked out, and heard this strange sound emanating from the toilet, *"Blu...blurp!"* I looked back in; the water was rising quickly and I could tell I was in for it. Water poured over the bowl, flooding the room like I was on the Titanic. I reached for the plunger, but there was no plunger. I just remember saying, *"No, no, no!"* This, apparently, doesn't stop water from running. Shutting off the water valve does. Now I'm in an inch of not-so-fresh-water. Eventually, I get my wits about me and clean it up. Needless to say, I was a bit more awake than just 15 minutes earlier. I didn't even want to walk upstairs for fear the furnace might explode! When I finally climbed into bed, my wife fast asleep, it occurred to me that as crazy as life had just been, I had contributed in some small way to my family's *wholeness*.

"Wholeness" or the Hebrew word, *shalom*, is a centerpiece of the entire biblical story and a fitting way to complete this *Multiply* journey. More than simply the absence of conflict, biblical shalom speaks of a completeness, a satisfying orderliness, a sense of glad fullness, where everything is as it should be, *flourishing* as God in His infinite wisdom intended. When a tree branch is hanging low because of the weight of ripe, fresh oranges, that's shalom. When a baby is nestled down, breathing slowly in her mama's arms, that's shalom. When a casted broken arm is finally set free and movement is regained, that is shalom. When a husband owns his sin with his wife and she forgives, that is shalom. You might experience a taste of it in a sunset over the ocean, or through an encouraging note that arrives at just the right moment. Shalom fills the air as a fair verdict is handed down, or as your whole family sits down to enjoy a lovingly prepared home-cooked meal. It's that exhilarating moment of hitting the game-winner at the buzzer, or receiving your diploma or commendation from your boss. These are all *glimpses*, moments of shalom breaking into our shattered world.

In the beginning, shalom permeated the Garden in Eden, and we are graciously promised in John's Revelation that it will be the *only* and *constant* and *lasting* experience in the New World. Can you imagine?

But what about in the *meantime*?

Well, this is where King Jesus and we, His multiplying disciples, come in. Alongside of shalom there is another common theme in Scripture and that is: *exile*. An exile is a foreigner or a refugee in a new land. Sadly, an exile often finds him or herself in unfamiliar territory, having been displaced from home against their will. Captivity is frequently involved, but not always. You can gladly move to a new city for business, yet feel very much like an exile. The smells are different, the tastes, the dialect, the values...etc. At least initially, being an exile is almost always an *anti-shalom* experience. Things don't fit, because *you* don't fit. There's loss and grief, anonymity and isolation. "Shalom" is like the exhale of walking into your home after a long, hard day.

Exile is like feeling homeless *even* where you live.

In the biblical story, the people of Israel found themselves in exile a fair amount. Once delivered from Egyptian exile and having settled down in the Promised Land, their eventual fixation with idolatry resulted in a sobering return to the misery of exile—the North (Israel) banished to Assyria, the South (Judah) to Babylon. In each case, God's people had an important decision to make. In fact, every exile is faced with the same choice: *"Do we make peace with what is and lean forward into the culture, bringing about shalom where we are, or do we pull back and tuck in; quarantining ourselves from potential pollutants, creating our own little experience of shalom while we await the exile's end?"* Preserving personal uniqueness might lead one to avoid societal integration. Such self-segregation, however, makes it highly unlikely that one will ever make a positive contribution.

And we're *made* for such contributions.

With His people at a crossroads, God spoke a surprising missional word through the prophet Jeremiah: *"Seek the welfare of the city where I have sent you into exile, and pray to the LORD on its behalf, for in its welfare you will find your welfare"* (Jeremiah 29:7). The word translated "welfare" is the Hebrew word *"shalom."* While God is eager for His people to remain set apart and distinct from the pagan culture into which He has sent them, He is equally eager for them to engage the world where they are and contribute to its wholeness. Even promising that, in the city's wholeness, they would experience theirs. God sent them there for a purpose. This is as applicable today for Jesus' disciples as it was for the exiles in Babylon. According to Scripture

we are exiles in the world.

Once you receive Gospel grace and bow your knee to King Jesus, you become a citizen of another kingdom—*His* kingdom, while you maintain your address here in the kingdom of this world. In Colossians 1:13-14 Paul explains, *"He (God the Father) has delivered us from the domain of darkness and transferred us to the Kingdom of His beloved Son, in whom we have redemption, the forgiveness of sins."* So we're a part of the light already, but we still navigate a world of darkness. Similarly, in Philippians 3:20 we learn that *"our citizenship is in heaven, and from it we await a Savior, the Lord Jesus Christ."* Until Jesus returns we live here, but our ultimate allegiance, our source of identity and security, is held in eternity. So how then shall we live? Well, the same way as God called Israel to live through the prophet Jeremiah.

Set *apart*, but leaning *in.*

In 1 Peter 2:11-12 the apostle Peter champions this perspective: *"Beloved, I urge you as sojourners and exiles to abstain from the passions of the flesh, which wage war against your soul. Keep your conduct among the Gentiles honorable, so that when they speak against you as evildoers, they may see your good deeds and glorify God on the day of visitation."* Peter assumes two things. First, while we are here we should be engaged with the broken world around us, and not aloof or indifferent. And secondly, our holy and honorable engagement will likely have a positive impact on real lives. While we must certainly avoid embracing the elements of the world that oppose God, we must not avoid embracing the people of the world altogether. After all, isn't it this very broken world that the Father loved so much that He willingly gave His only Son? And isn't it into this world that King Jesus himself prayerfully sent His disciples, of which we are now numbered: *"I do not ask you to take them out of the world...as you sent me into the world, so I have sent them into the world"* (John 17:15, 18)? We are not in the world by accident. You live, you work, and you play where you do for a reason.

So, *life* is mission.

Now, being in the world doesn't license us to embrace its destructive folly, but we need not avoid the darkness completely in order to remain faithful. In fact, it's as we are faithful to Jesus in the midst of the brokenness of this world that we can contribute to its restoration. You are a shalom-bearer everywhere you go. *That* is an amazing thought. Originally, we were image-bearers called by God to be fruitful and to multiply and to fill the earth with His glory. Yet, out of the gate we lost our way. Thankfully God pursued. And now, as the redeemed, we are recommissioned to our original task, with more clarity than ever. As God restores wholeness in us through Gospel grace and the indwelling presence of the Holy Spirit, we can freely live honorable lives chock-full of good deeds, which will likely result in some giving glory to God.

This may not be our eternal home, but it *is* where God has us. Will we just survive, or will we thrive? Will we put our heads in the sand and hand this world over to ever-increasing brokenness, or follow in Jesus' incarnational footsteps, embracing our exile as an opportunity to bring wholeness? King Jesus may appear tomorrow, and we pray that He does, but if He delays as a mercy to the future disciples around us, let's joyfully seek their welfare in everyday, tangible ways. Instead of merely pining for the promised new world, let's contribute to the flourishing of people in the meantime. We may not belong here, but we know to whom we belong. And so we of all people ought to be most free.

Let's live *on purpose.*

Let's participate in King Jesus' on-going mission in His world. Let's settle down and settle in. Let's work and shop and volunteer and play. Let's host neighbors, care for laborers, relieve single-parents, encourage the aging, engage the forgotten, and give hope to the hopeless. Let's marshal all of our creative ingenuity and efforts, personally and corporately, as the King's literal Body on earth, bringing Gospel restoration to the precious lives around us. They don't know how much they matter to the One who made them. We do! So, with grace in hand, inspired and empowered by the Spirit within, for God's glory and the lasting joy of all people, let's *multiply*!

The Gospel

In the midst of the personal heartache that we all live with at some level, and in the face of all the pain and evil in the world, not to mention the uncertainties of the future, wouldn't it be reassuring to know that there is some *good* news? Everyday we're bombarded with the reminder that things are broken and that there's little hope of them ever getting better. But what if we discovered that there *is* hope, that wholeness and restoration are possible?

Wouldn't that make *all* the difference in the world?

GOD'S PURPOSE

We believe that there is One God, who created all things (Genesis 1:1, Isaiah 45:12, John 1:3, Colossians 1:16)—like birds and oceans, roses and trout. And the greatest thing He created was us (Genesis 1:26-27, Psalm 139:13-16). You and me. People. Everything else in creation is for our provision—nourishment and enjoyment— a place to live and work and play (Genesis 1:28-30). This perfect, always loving, always good, always worthy God made us to *know* Him. He wants us to know who He is and what He's like. He made us to *love* Him, not because He needs love, but because in relationship with Him, we discover His love, which satisfies our deepest longings. This One God made us to *worship* Him—to make much of Him. Again, not because He needs worship, but because He's the only God worthy of worship, and we are most alive when we acknowledge that. The God who made you, made you to *trust* Him, like a loving, faithful Father who always keeps His promises (Psalm 86:15).

No one is *worthy* of your trust like God.

And just like we are often chips off the old block, God made us to be just like Him. Not to replace Him, but to *reflect* His character in how we relate to one another. God's intention, His purpose was to create a people who knew Him, loved Him, worshipped Him, trusted Him, and reflected Him throughout His creation. He started with one couple, Adam and Eve. Sadly, however, it didn't take long for them to choose their own way, walking away from the One who made them.

That **decision has impacted us all.**

OUR CONDITION

Adam and Eve began to doubt God's goodness, shirking His authority in their lives. They wanted to do what they wanted, their way, and on their time. Sound a little familiar? It's a rebellious posture we often identify with kids as the "terrible two's." But that heart posture is in all of us. Call it selfishness, call it pride; it is a rejection of God and God's design, and God calls it "sin." It is anything in us that falls short of that for which God made us. Like a product that gets recalled for malfunction, we malfunctioned out of the gate when we made ourselves into miniature "gods." Now each one of us enters this world broken, longing, disappointed, and discouraged. We don't know *who* we are because we don't know *who's* we are! We're missing this all-important relationship with God, and that skews everything in life—our passions, our pursuits, our purpose.

And *no one* **is immune.**

Even the seemingly most kind and gentle among us have ourselves at the heart of our motivation (Romans 3:10-12, 23). *This* is a sobering reality check, but it explains the corruption of our world. Things are not as they're supposed to be. They're off, out of joint, awry. Every day reminds us of this. And we would remain hopeless unless God graciously chose to do something about this mess we've created. The good news is, He has!

GOD'S PROVISION

Even in the face of our rebellion, God gladly made great promises. As Adam and Eve were removed from God's presence, God gave a promise that one day a son of Eve would overcome the tempting threat of evil in this world (Genesis 3:15). Through a man named Abraham, God promised to bring blessing to all the nations of the earth through Abraham's lineage—Israel (Genesis 12:1-3). God delivered Israel from Egyptian captivity (Exodus 12:33-42, 14:1ff), a dramatic foreshadowing of God delivering us all from captivity to sin. In time God sent prophets to Israel promising that a day was coming when He would graciously intervene. A son would be born to a virgin, who would be *Immanuel*—"God with us" (Isaiah 7:14, 9:6,). And through His unjust suffering at our hands, He would sacrificially take all of our sin upon Himself (Isaiah 53:5-6, 1 Peter 2:22-24). He would offer us a peace we could never know apart from Him and set us free from sin's *penalty*, which is death, and sin's *power* in our lives. God kept His promise! In the first century that son arrived, and He was given the name Jesus,

"the One who *saves.*"
(Matthew 1:21-23)

Jesus was God in person (John 1:1-3, 14, 18). Fully God, yet truly one of us. He enjoyed a relationship with God the Father that we were made for. He modeled it. And He loved. Oh, how He *loved!* Everywhere He went, Jesus pursued the rebel and loved the unlovable. Those who thought their sin was too great, discovered that no sin was too great for Jesus. Our sin is precisely why He came. God was passionately, relentlessly pursuing people through Jesus. And that pursuit culminated in Him laying down His own life—like a good shepherd would for His own sheep (John 10:11, 14-15, 17-18)—suffering a Roman cross, dying, and being buried in a tomb. For three days, the tomb held Him. But on Easter Sunday the power of death gave out, and Jesus rose from the dead (1 Corinthians 15:1-4)! Not just back to the life He lost, but through death and out the other side into a newness of life no one, to this day, has ever known.

Resurrection **life.**

A new body, animated by God's Spirit, unable to suffer disease or death again. And now Jesus is uniquely qualified to offer us life (John 11:25-26). But we all have a choice to make.

OUR RESPONSE

There are two paths. Like Adam and Eve in the beginning, we can choose to continue on our own path—living life as we see fit, searching hopelessly, looking to possessions, or positions, to experiences or people to satisfy the lingering ache we all know so well. Sometimes it is satisfying, but it never seems to last. You ever notice that? There's always a need for new, for more, for something…*else*.

That's life on our *own* path.

And sadly it ends in death (Romans 6:23). If in this life we do not know God, we will have no desire or opportunity to know Him beyond this life. And thirsty, hungry, and unsatisfied become the hallmarks of life beyond death. Forever.

But there is *another* way.

Jesus has opened for us a new way into life, a new way to live (John 14:6). A life where sins are always forgiven—every sin you've ever committed and all those just up ahead. No sin too great. Imagine a life where you are *adopted* by the One who made you (Romans 8:15-16, Galatians 4:4-7, Ephesians 1:5). A forever family. No more wondering if you belong, if you can be known, if you're included. You are. *Always*. And no more loneliness. A life where God's very own presence delights to dwell within you by His Holy Spirit (John 14:16-17, Romans 8:9, 1 Corinthians 6:19). The very same Spirit that led Jesus when He lived on the earth. Think of it. *Access* to the Living God 24/7. In your bedroom, in your car, at the office, in the store, there's no place where you would roam away from His presence. His wisdom, available. His guidance, always. And His strength. The Spirit strengthens you from within to not only *know* what God wants for you, but to begin to *want* what He wants and to pursue what He wants (Philippians 2:13). This is what you were made for. But we malfunctioned, remember?

It's God's *grace* that puts us
back together **again.**

We can't do anything to make things right between us and God. But God *can* make things right. In fact, He already has through Jesus (Romans 5:6-11).

So which path will it be? The one you're used to, that you cling to only because it's familiar, not because it's satisfying. Or Jesus' path? The trail He lovingly blazed *for* you. A path that leads to life. A full, meaningful life of growing love for God and for others in *this* life (Matthew 22:34-40), and the promise of life with God and with God's people forever!?

Like any journey, if you get lost, you often have to turn around to move in the right direction. That "turn" is called *repentance* (Romans 2:4). It starts with acknowledging your sin: *"I have lived my life for myself instead of for You, God."* And then you receive His grace by faith (Ephesians 2:8-9) and say "yes" to God's new way of life led by His Spirit. None of us knows at the beginning all that that will mean, but a full "turn" includes a yielding of your will to God's will. It is an invitation for Him to have His way in your life, more and more.

For all of us there are ups and downs along the way, times when we feel close to God and times when we wonder where He is. He'll always be right there with you. There will be times when you have clarity on what He wants and you'll delight to obey Him, but then there will also be times when it is not clear, or times when you will choose steps from the old path. Those are mirages. They don't hold out life. Thankfully, there is great grace available for you all along the journey. Every day (Lamentations 3:22-23). God offers you forgiveness whenever you ask (1 John 1:9), and will graciously reorient you back to the life He has in store for you. What do you say, your path, or His?

Faith in *yourself,* **or faith in** *God***?**

If it's faith in God, you might begin that journey with a prayer like this:

> *"Father, I don't know all that it will mean, but I want to say 'Yes!' to you. I know that I have lived for myself, that I have sinned against you and others, and I am sorry. Would you please forgive me? I say 'Yes!' to your conviction in my heart. I thank you for the gift of your Son, Jesus, who laid down His life for me and rose again to give me new life. I say 'Yes!' to your grace through Jesus Christ my Lord. And I say 'Yes!' to the new way of Your Spirit. Fill me, change me, and use me for your purposes and your glory. I want to grow to love you and to love others. Help me, Father. Thank you. I love you. Amen."*

GOD'S PROMISE

To everyone who believes, God holds out this amazing promise regarding the *future*: our new life-giving relationship with Him will never end. *Ever* (John 3:16). Nothing, not even death, which brings this physical life to a close...nothing can ever separate you from God's loving presence (Romans 8:38-39). The moment you close your eyes in this life, you will open them anew in the life to come (Luke 23:43, Philippians 1:21-24). In Heaven you will be present with Jesus, satisfied, exhaled, at peace, at rest.

Everything *just...right.*

And there's more! Life with Jesus immediately upon death, but then this promise: a day is coming when Jesus will return (John 14:1-3, 1 Thessalonians 2:19)! Just as God promised long ago that He would come and in Jesus He did, so God promises that Jesus, who now reigns in Heaven, will return one final time to bring justice to the earth He created (2 Thessalonians 1:5-12). Any lingering evil or sin will be dealt with swiftly and fairly. Those who refuse God's provision of Jesus in this life, will find themselves acknowledging their grave mistake when He returns. They'll remain in rebellion and move on with their lives in torment as their rejection of Jesus will find no end. They will have chosen Hell…for themselves.

But for those who are waiting (2 Timothy 4:8), Jesus' return will mean great rejoicing, a massive party like a wedding feast for the greatest of royals (Revelation 19:6-10). A feast without end. God's presence finally and fully on the earth (Revelation 21:3). His presence filling every nook and cranny of His New Creation.

No more **sin.**
No more **dying.**
No more **pain.**
No more **grief.**
Only *joy.*
(Revelation 21:4)

And sweet reunion with those we love, who love God, living in a restored Creation! Everything just as it should be. Justice. Righteousness. Everything just…right.

Does your heart not *long* for that day!?

There *is* good news! The greatest news ever! News that radically alters the course of one's life when it is heard and believed. Males and females, young and old, rich and poor; Asians, Africans, Hispanics, Europeans, Americans…you name it! *Anyone* who calls upon the name of the Lord Jesus will be *saved* (Romans 10:9-13), and will find great joy and hope welling up within them. Anyone. Which includes you!

So, *your* **path or** *God's***?**

Receive God's grace through Jesus Christ and you will live. And when you do, tell someone who knows Christ soon, so that they can encourage you and direct you to the next steps in your new walk of faith. Let the journey begin!

Made in the USA
Lexington, KY
25 August 2017